UNLAWFUL ORDERS

UNLAWFUL ORDERS

A Portrait of Dr. James B. Williams, Tuskegee Airman, Surgeon, and Activist

BARBARA BINNS

SCHOLASTIC
FOCUS | NEW YORK

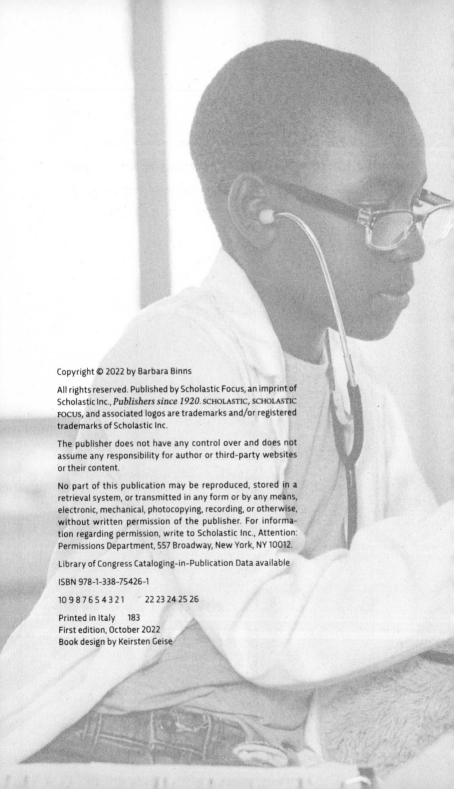

All rights reserved. Published by Scholastic Focus, an imprint of Scholastic Inc., *Publishers since 1920.* SCHOLASTIC, SCHOLASTIC FOCUS, and associated logos are trademarks and/or registered trademarks of Scholastic Inc.

The publisher does not have any control over and does not assume any responsibility for author or third-party websites or their content.

Library of Congress Cataloging-in-Publication Data available

ISBN 978-1-338-75426-1

10 9 8 7 6 5 4 3 2 1   22 23 24 25 26

Printed in Italy   183
First edition, October 2022
Book design by Keirsten Geise

For all the determined Black men and women serving the world in the military, as teachers and health care professionals, and, most of all, as good parents raising the next generation of heroes

CONTENTS

CONTENTS

INTRODUCTION

HISTORY OVERFLOWS WITH STORIES of men and women who seem larger than life. Many appear to have been born knowing they would change the future. But sometimes, very ordinary people make major differences in the world. Look in the mirror and you may see a future Clara Belle Williams, Esteban Hotesse, Coleman Young, or Benjamin O. Davis. Or a future Dr. James Buchanan Williams, known as JB to his friends.

I chose to look at the extraordinary life of James B. Williams because he accomplished many things that improve the lives of people today. He didn't just live through twentieth-century American history. He helped create it. While studying his life, I quickly discovered that there is no experience like trying to research a man named Williams. Go on, try it, I double-dare you.

Fortunately, the women in James Williams's life came to my rescue. His mother, Clara Belle Williams, achieved fame in her own right. As a scholarship winner, this daughter of slaves became the first member of her family to attend college. She then became a teacher and continued her own education to become the first Black person to graduate with a bachelor of science degree from New Mexico State University. Although she originally faced segregation at NMSU, the university eventually came to see her as a beloved alum, honoring her tenacity and determination with an honorary doctorate. Not only did NMSU rename the English building after her, they now house a trove of documents about her and her family.

Another valuable source of information on James Williams was his daughter, Brenda Payton Jones. Her prolific career as a journalist made her information easier to research. Several of her articles provided details of her parents and grandparents. As a side note, Brenda and I grew up near each other in Chicago, so close we might have passed on the Hyde Park sidewalks. We could have ended up in the same school, except I attended Hyde Park High School (now the Hyde Park Academy High School) while she entered the University of Chicago Laboratory School, a place I only wished I could afford to attend.

We came so close, and yet remained so far apart.

Other sources for this book include interviews with his grandson Dr. James B. Williams II, news items, and video and oral histories collected from several members of the 477th Bombardment Group made before they died. Many of those men were considered local heroes after World War II. Still others entered politics or achieved fame in their chosen professions. The military picked only the best for the Tuskegee Airmen program, and the men continued to shine throughout their lives. While most are now deceased—JB died in 2016 at the age of ninety-seven—

the obituaries of these heroes also proved to be information troves.

I grew up near Hyde Park, which means I walked down some of the same streets members of the Williams family once trod. My sister, a former nurse, told me stories about both Dr. Jasper and Dr. James Williams and their South Side clinic. By the time I finished my research, I felt honored to write about the Williams family, ordinary people turned extraordinary. I hope you feel the same while reading about them.

Final note: During the time of this story, the early and mid-twentieth century, the terms used for people of African descent were Negro or Colored. In fact, I grew up being called Colored. For the most part, I use today's terminology, Black or African American, depending on which seems most relevant to the moment. When I directly quote a document or speech from the time period, I use the words that person used. Otherwise, I use today's terms, both as a personal habit and reference to the changing times, and as a sign of respect to what these men and women achieved with their lives.

MEET JB WILLIAMS

On October 31, 1907, a Black man named Alex Johnson was arrested in Cameron, Texas. The charge: attempting to assault a white woman. Those kinds of accusations usually brought automatic death sentences with no evidence or proof of guilt required.

When word spread that Johnson would not receive the death penalty, hundreds of white people assembled around the jail. The mob used sledgehammers to break down jail doors and remove the prisoner. According to newspapers, the unstoppable, bloodthirsty crowd meant to have Mr. Johnson at any cost. The mob of

The SHAME of AMERICA

Do you know that the United States is the Only Land on Earth where human beings are BURNED AT THE STAKE?

In Five Years 1918-1922, Thirty-six People were publicly BURNED BY AMERICAN MOBS

60 Persons were lynched in 1922

3496 PEOPLE LYNCHED, 1889-1922

For What Crimes Have Mobs Nullified Government and Inflicted the Death Penalty?

The Alleged Crimes	The Victims	Why Some Mob Victims Died:
Murder	1,297	
Rape	591	Not turning out of road for white boy in auto
Attacks on women	263	Being a relative of a person who was lynched
Crimes against the person	364	Jumping a labor contract
Crimes against property	334	Being a member of the Non-Partisan League
Miscellaneous crimes	463	"Talking Back" to a white man
Absence of crime	184	"Insulting" white man
	3,496	

Is Rape the "Cause" of Lynching?

Of 3,496 people murdered by mobs in our country, only 591, or less than 17 per cent, were even accused of the crime of rape.

83 WOMEN HAVE BEEN LYNCHED IN THE UNITED STATES

Do lynchers maintain that they were lynched for "the usual crime?"

AND THE LYNCHERS GO UNPUNISHED

THE REMEDY

The Dyer Anti-Lynching Bill is Still Before the United States Senate

The Dyer Anti-Lynching Bill was passed on January 26, 1922, by a vote of 230 to 119 in the House of Representatives

The Dyer Anti-Lynching Bill Provides:

That culpable State officers and mobbists shall be tried in Federal Courts on failure of State courts to act, and that a county in which a lynching occurs shall be fined $10,000, recoverable in a Federal Court.

The Principal Objection Advanced Against the Bill is upon the Ground of Constitutionality.

The Constitutionality of the Dyer Bill Has Been Affirmed by

The Judiciary Committee of the House of Representatives

The Judiciary Committee of the Senate

The United States Attorney General, legal adviser of Congress

Judge Guy D. Goff, of the Department of Justice

The Senate has been petitioned to pass the Dyer Bill by

29 Lawyers and Jurists including two former Attorney Generals of the United States

19 State Supreme Court Justices

24 State Governors

3 Archbishops, 85 bishops and prominent churchmen

39 Mayors of large cities, north and south

The American Bar Association at its meeting in San Francisco, August 9, 1922, adopted a resolution asking for further legislation by Congress to punish and prevent lynching and mob violence.

Fifteen State Conventions of 1922 (3 of them Democratic) have inserted in their party platforms a demand for national action to stamp out lynchings.

Lynching Creates Unrest. It Stimulated Northward Migration of Negro Workers from the South. It Injures Agriculture and Lessens Productiveness of Labor.

THE DYER ANTI-LYNCHING BILL IS STILL BEFORE THE SENATE TELEGRAPH YOUR SENATORS YOU WANT IT ENACTED

If you want to help the organization which has brought to light the facts about lynching, the organization which is fighting for 100 per cent Americanism, not for some of the people some of the time, but for all of the people, white or black, all of the time.

Send your check to J. E. SPINGARN, Treasurer of the

National Association for the Advancement of Colored People

70 FIFTH AVENUE, NEW YORK CITY

An anti-lynching poster issued by the National Association for the Advancement of Colored People.

angry white men moved "like the swollen stream of a mountain." Anyone who tried to stop them would have been killed. Not even the sheriff tried to intervene.

Huddled behind the locked doors of his nearby medical office, Dr. Aaron Nixon could only listen in horror as Johnson cried while being tortured. Meanwhile, white spectators pulled out chairs and sat on the balconies of surrounding buildings to watch their victim being led across the courtyard to a large oak tree and lynched. The newspapers deemed the crowd "orderly."

Johnson's death was one of many lynchings that occurred in the area, and it was enough to make Dr. Nixon and his college friend, teacher Jasper Buchanan Williams, decide it was time to leave Cameron. Both men held a special hatred for the lynching of Black people that occurred year after year. Jasper Williams burned with a passion for civil rights. He was described as a "driving, ambitious man who realized much was wrong with society."

They moved to El Paso, a place called Sun City that was rumored to be slightly less hostile to Black people.

Jasper may have had a personal reason for choosing El Paso as his new home. Clara Belle Drisdale, a former Cameron teacher and his future wife, now taught in El Paso.

Clara Belle Drisdale was born in Plum, Texas, in 1885, the eldest child of sharecroppers and former slaves. Sharecroppers farmed land owned by someone else, using a portion of the crops to pay for rent and the cost of seeds and other supplies. Sharecropping could be a good way for people with limited start-up funds to make a beginning, *if* the landowner was fair. The Drisdale family was lucky. The man who owned their land was fair in his accounting of their debts and payments. Besides, Clara Belle admitted years later, as a child she sometimes leaned on the scales just a tiny bit when it was time to weigh the crops she'd gathered to gain a little extra money.

Her family took the name Drisdale from their former owners. Her father never attended school but taught himself to read and write with an old spelling

Clara Belle Drisdale Williams.

book, and her mother learned her ABC's. Clara Belle was the eldest of five in a family that wanted their children educated at any cost. When she was a small child, her grandfather bounced her on his lap while boasting, "This is going to be my little school-teacher." Maybe he saw the future, or perhaps he inspired her, because education—and her family—became Clara Belle's life.

She had to work long hours on the family farm while also caring for her younger brothers and sisters. Somehow, she still found time to study. Her belief in education as a key to success won her a scholarship to Prairie View Normal and Industrial College (now Prairie View A&M University). The scholarship covered about half her tuition and room and board. She worked at the school to pay for the rest.

Filled with dedication, determination, and native intelligence, Clara Belle received a degree in home economics, the art and science of home management. She graduated at the age of nineteen as class valedictorian, a title given to the student with the best academic performance. Graduation was not a goodbye for her. Prairie View promptly hired her to lead their sewing department. She worked at the college for several years before moving to Cameron, where she taught in 1907 and first met Jasper Buchanan Williams.

Jasper wrote her every month after she left Cameron. They grew closer when he moved to El Paso, too, in 1909. Thus began a long courtship. Jasper felt he should not marry until he finished helping his younger siblings complete their educations.

He and Dr. Nixon helped found the El Paso chapter of the National Association for the Advancement of Colored People (NAACP). At a time when many Texas NAACP chapters experienced a decline, the El Paso chapter flourished. Jasper Williams served as the chapter's first president, a role that earned him numerous threats, many from Ku Klux Klan members. The KKK is a white supremacist hate group formed after the Civil War. Members hid their identities under white hoods when they went out to set fires, bomb, kill, and terrorize innocent people. Klan members in Cameron likely made up the majority of the mob that murdered Mr. Johnson. Many of El Paso's prominent citizens, including lawyers, politicians, bankers, businessmen, and teachers, were not-so-secret Klan members. That was one reason Jasper Buchanan kept a firearm under his pillow and carried it with him whenever he left his home.

Once his younger siblings finished school, Jasper proposed to Clara Belle—on NAACP stationery! They married in 1917, left teaching, and purchased the Williams Drug Store, where they worked together while starting a family.

The couple had three sons, Jasper Fleming Williams in 1918, James Buchanan Williams in 1919, and Charles Lee Williams in 1923. Dr. Nixon delivered all three at the Williams's home. By this time, Dr. Nixon was considered one of El Paso's top physicians. But it was also a time when Black doctors were automatically considered substandard. That did not keep numerous white and Mexican patients from coming to see him in his office for treatment. But it did keep hospitals from ever agreeing to put him or any other Black doctor on their staff or grant him the right to admit patients.

The middle son, James Buchanan, was often called JB by his friends. JB's birth came during a period marked by the armistice ending World War I, the so-called war to end all wars that would make the world safe for democracy, and the bloody Red Summer, when many Black veterans of that war were forced to take up arms at home.

WORLD WAR I

BLACK AMERICANS HAVE ALWAYS fought, or tried to fight, for their country. At the beginning of the Revolutionary War, George Washington and other slave owners opposed the idea of allowing Black men in the army (even though some slave owners sent slaves to fight in order to avoid being drafted themselves). The British promised freedom to any enslaved man or woman who escaped and joined their side. Thousands responded. That, plus a lack of manpower in the Continental army, changed things. Too few white men chose to leave their farms and families to fight. Washington had to agree to allow Black recruitment, often with the offer of freedom as an inducement.

The result was a fully integrated army. Records reveal that there were between five and eight thousand "Colored" members of the Continental army. Black and white soldiers drilled together. They fought, ate, slept, starved, marched, and died side by side. Men of each race depended on each other to survive and eventually win independence—for white colonists. This led to some Northerners questioning how the new America could call for freedom for themselves while enslaving others. That bolstered the growing abolitionist movement.

When the British army withdrew, they kept their promise, evacuating more than three thousand former slaves as free men and women. The enslaved soldiers who'd fought for Washington were sent back to slaveholders, who conveniently forgot the promises of freedom. When the time came to dole out veterans' benefits, the new United States government ignored its Black veterans.

This pattern repeated in future wars. Northern Blacks stepped up and volunteered for the Civil War, looking for freedom and respect. Union recruiters turned them away until casualties left a shortage of white soldiers. That led to the formation of 163 regiments consisting of 200,000 Black soldiers in Union blue. When the Civil War ended, their efforts for their country were again forgotten.

When the United States entered World War I, Black men and women once again rushed to volunteer as soldiers and nurses. Many considered the war a god-sent blessing, one they hoped would let them prove they deserved respect. Intellectual leaders like W. E. B. Du Bois thought fighting for America would be like paying a voluntary blood tax and help change the way Black people were perceived and treated in the United States.

On the other hand, white officials like Mississippi senator James K. Vardaman sounded an alarm as early as 1917. He warned that if you "impress the Negro with the fact that he is defending the flag" and "inflate his untutored soul with military airs," he might begin to believe that "his political rights must be respected."

Black nurses, eager to assist in the war effort, attempted to enlist in the Army Nurse Corps. They were turned away. "Don't let it be said by the great American historians in the coming years that only the American white women served as nurses in the great conflict . . . put in a paragraph that the colored woman wanted to go but we wouldn't let her," wrote an anonymous commenter in *The Baltimore Afro-American*. Unfortunately, that wish largely went forgotten until the 1918 flu pandemic did what the war could not and finally forced the army to admit Black nurses. Those nurses helped save soldiers in Ohio at Camps Sherman and Grant. At the same time, however, the dean of Ohio's Hiram College refused to let a Black nurse care for influenza victims at the college.

Black men faced the same rejection. No American general agreed to accept Black soldiers as fighting men. So they fought for the French.

Twenty-six-year-old Henry Johnson, a New York railway porter, joined the all-Black 15th New York National Guard Regiment. Theodore Roosevelt Jr. called the

Picket station of Colored troops near Dutch Gap Canal, Virginia.

Black private "one of the five bravest American soldiers in the war."

The 15th New York National Guard Regiment was composed of Black men who wanted to serve their country and fight the enemy overseas. Some came from as far away as Texas to sign up. The regiment tried and failed to find a home as a fighting unit among US troops.

National Guard units from across the country were organized into a single division that then-major Douglas MacArthur said would stretch like a rainbow. New York's 69th Infantry Regiment, primarily composed of Irish Americans, was accepted as part of that Rainbow Division. The 15th was not. When they applied to join so they could be trained with the other regiments, they were told that "black was not a color of the rainbow."

Imagine being one of the many Black men rushing to enlist, filled with patriotism and a desire to fight for your country, capable of facing the enemy as an equal to white soldiers. Then, once you are an enlisted man, they thrust a shovel into your hands instead of a rifle

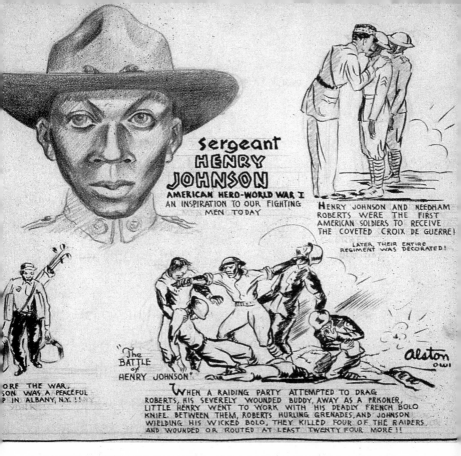

Text within the illustration:

Sergeant
HENRY JOHNSON
AMERICAN HERO—WORLD WAR I
AN INSPIRATION TO OUR FIGHTING
MEN TODAY

HENRY JOHNSON AND NEEDHAM ROBERTS WERE THE FIRST AMERICAN SOLDIERS TO RECEIVE THE COVETED CROIX DE GUERRE!

LATER, THEIR ENTIRE REGIMENT WAS DECORATED!

"The BATTLE of HENRY JOHNSON"

ORE THE WAR, SON WAS A PEACEFUL P IN ALBANY, N.Y.!!

WHEN A RAIDING PARTY ATTEMPTED TO DRAG ROBERTS, HIS SEVERELY WOUNDED BUDDY, AWAY AS A PRISONER, LITTLE HENRY WENT TO WORK WITH HIS DEADLY FRENCH BOLO KNIFE. BETWEEN THEM, ROBERTS HURLING GRENADES, AND JOHNSON WIELDING HIS WICKED BOLO, THEY KILLED FOUR OF THE RAIDERS AND WOUNDED OR ROUTED AT LEAST TWENTY FOUR MORE!!

Alston OWI

SGT. HENRY JOHNSON—AMERICAN HERO of WORLD WAR I—AN INSPIRATION TO OUR FIGHTING MEN TODAY by Charles Henry Alston.

and tell you your job is ditchdigger. Or being pointed to the cook tent and told your only weapon is a knife to use when peeling potatoes. Black soldiers became truck drivers and stevedores, and they were assigned tasks such as cleaning or digging ditches or latrines. Is it any wonder their morale plummeted?

Then the United States Army renamed the 15th New York National Guard to the 369th Infantry and turned the group over to France. The American generals basically said, take them, we're not using them anyway. The French rushed to accept the 369th and several additional Black Infantry regiments. The French ranks already included hundreds of thousands of *armée noire*, the nickname given to troops France recruited from sub-Saharan Africa to fight at the front.

The French gave the men respect they had never found in America. France handed members of the 369th French helmets, French weapons, and taught them enough French words to understand commands before stationing the men on the front line.

Private Henry Johnson stood five feet four on his tiptoes and weighed 130 pounds. He was posted at the western edge of the Argonne Forest, in the Champagne region of France. On May 15, 1918, he and another American, Needham Roberts, age seventeen, were given sentry duty on the graveyard shift, midnight to four a.m. He thought it was "crazy" to send untrained men out, he later told a reporter, but he agreed to "tackle the job."

Around two in the morning, he heard what he called the "snippin' and clippin'" of wire cutters on the perimeter fence. He hurled a grenade at the noise. That brought a volley of return gunfire and enemy grenades. Bullets and shrapnel ripped through the men. Roberts was wounded too badly to fight or run for assistance. He lay in the trench and handed Johnson grenades to toss. When Johnson and Roberts ran out of grenades, Germans advanced on them from every direction. Johnson was hit by bullets again and again, but he kept firing his rifle into the darkness. The men had received very little training. That's one reason why, while reloading his French rifle, Johnson accidentally shoved in an American cartridge clip. The gun jammed.

As the Germans closed in, Johnson swung his rifle like a champion baseball player, knocking them back until the rifle stock splintered. When he saw Germans trying to drag Roberts away, he reached for the only weapon he had left, a bolo knife. He had to save his

African troops with a machine gun during an exercise in World War I from a photographic postcard, 1915.

comrade from capture by the Germans. The men had already agreed death was better than capture. Johnson now decided victory would be best of all.

He charged, exposing himself to even more danger in order to engage enemy soldiers in hand-to-hand combat. He thrust the knife through one German soldier's head. He stabbed another in the stomach, nearly disemboweling him, and he drove the bolo knife between the ribs of yet another German who tried to climb on his back.

"Each slash meant something, believe me," Johnson said later. "I wasn't doing exercises, let me tell you." He continued hacking at the Germans with a ferocity that made them panic and drop Roberts. The sound of advancing French and American forces sent the surviving Germans running back into the darkness. Almost single-handedly, Henry Johnson had successfully kept the German force from breaking through the French line. Although he suffered twenty-one wounds, he killed four Germans and wounded over ten more. The enemy failed to secure prisoners because of his bravery and determination to keep his comrade safe.

"There wasn't anything so fine about it," he said later. "Just fought for my life. A rabbit would have done that." He gained the nickname "Black Death," a plague against the German enemies.

One effect of his ferocity was increased vigilance and confidence among the men of the 369th Infantry Regiment. They went on to win acclaim as the Harlem Hellfighters and spent 191 days under fire without ever losing a foot of ground or having a man taken prisoner. The Hellfighters also introduced France to live jazz music from a regimental band led by infantry officer and all-star bandleader James Reese Europe. Europe traveled to Puerto Rico, where he recruited numerous musicians for the band. Many of the Puerto Rican musicians settled in New York after the war. That included internationally celebrated composer Rafael Hernández, a man who changed the face of Latin music in the US following the war. Rafael Hernández went on to become one of the most important composers of Puerto Rican popular music in the twentieth century.

The entire French force stationed in Champagne lined up to watch Johnson and Roberts receive the Croix de Guerre, the French equivalent of the United States Medal of Honor. The medal given to the

The Harlem Hellfighters, Séchault, France, September 29, 1918.

Black Death included the Gold Palm, which is given for acts of extraordinary valor.

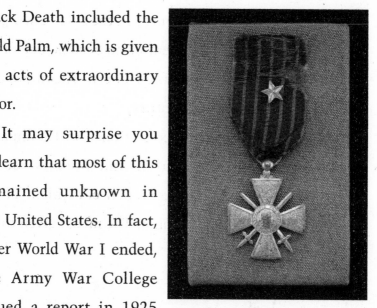

Croix de Guerre medal.

It may surprise you to learn that most of this remained unknown in the United States. In fact, after World War I ended, the Army War College issued a report in 1925 claiming the performance of Black soldiers during the war showed them to be "mentally inferior to the white man," "subservient" and "lackadaisical," and that they possessed no ability for leadership. They made no allowances for the lack of training given the men at the start of the war, or for how low morale must have sunk when men were not allowed to defend a country that belonged to them, too. There was no mention of heroes like the Black Death.

Members of the famous 369th Colored Infantry arrive in New York City.

Henry Johnson and Needham Roberts in 1918.

Most celebrations marking the end of World War I excluded even the mention of Black members of the military. Only New York celebrated its Hellfighters when Henry Johnson and the others returned, holding a parade for the heroes on February 17, 1919. By then he had earned a promotion to sergeant. Like hundreds of thousands of young American men returned from World War I, Johnson tried to make a life for himself. His discharge records erroneously made no mention of his injuries, denying him both a Purple Heart and a disability allowance. He resumed his job as a Red Cap Porter at a train station and tried to carry on. But he never overcame injuries that included a metal plate holding his shattered left foot together. His wife and three children left when he was unable to hold on to a job. He died, destitute and alone, in 1929 at the age of thirty-two. He is buried in Arlington National Cemetery in Arlington, Virginia.

In 1996, Johnson's family received the posthumous Purple Heart he deserved. The Distinguished

Service Cross was awarded in 2002, and in 2015, President Barack Obama presented his son Herman Johnson with his father's well-deserved Medal of Honor.

THE RED SUMMER OF 1919

As HARD AS THINGS were for Henry Johnson after he returned from the war, things were worse for many other Black veterans. June 28, 1919, brought the signing of the Treaty of Versailles, formally ending the war that was supposed to make the world safe for democracy. Never mind the world. America itself was unsafe, as many returning Black soldiers soon discovered. According to professor of African American history Simon Balto:

> *World War I was very much a broken promise for basically all African Americans, but the people*

*who felt the brokenness of that promise most
acutely [were the veterans] who had gone and
risked their lives for this supposed war to make
the world safe for democracy and then came home
to find that the country was still going to deny
African Americans the privilege of democracy.*

W. E. B. Du Bois wrote a prescient editorial about things to come in May 1919 entitled "Returning Soldiers." He ended the editorial by telling Black Americans:

*We are cowards and jackasses if now that the war
is over, we do not marshal every ounce of our
brain and brawn to fight a sterner, longer, more
unbending battle against the forces of hell in our
own land.*

We return.

We return from fighting.

We return fighting.

*Make way for democracy. We saved it in
France, and by the Great Jehovah, we will save*

it in the United States of America, or know the
reason why.

While they were overseas, many Black soldiers gained organizational skills and learned to be assertive. They returned knowing how to use weapons and carry themselves proudly in their uniforms—all things that undermined claims of racial superiority and infuriated many white Americans. That's why Black veterans were seen as a threat. Some were beaten or shot. Many, like Private Charles Lewis, were lynched while still in their uniform.

Private Lewis left Camp Sherman, in Chillicothe, Ohio, heading home to Alabama. He had his honorable discharge, along with documents from his commanding officers describing his excellent service record. The local deputy sheriff didn't care about any of that when he demanded the right to inspect the uniformed soldier's baggage. An argument broke out between the two men and Lewis was charged with assault and resisting arrest.

The next day, he was dead.

An August 2, 1919, illustration that appeared in the *Washington Bee*, a weekly newspaper based in Washington, DC, and founded and read by African Americans.

Masked men stormed the jail in the middle of the night, pulled the soldier from his cell, and hanged him. His body, still in uniform, was left dangling for all to see.

Within days of the murder of Private Lewis, the *True Democrat*, a Louisiana paper, published an editorial blaming him for his own death entitled "Nip It in the Bud." According to the editorial, the problem was that "the negro thought that being a soldier he was not subject to civil authority," so he had the nerve to think he was no longer required to obey every order a white man gave him. That idea made him "guilty of many acts of self-assertion, arrogance and insolence which will not be borne with, in the South at least . . . A line is set that divides them from the Southern whites which cannot be passed."

That line was crossed again and again during anti-Black uprisings in what became known as the Red Summer of 1919. The most violent of the uprisings

The front page of the African American weekly newspaper the *Chicago Defender*, August 2, 1919.

in the summer of 1919 occurred in Washington, DC; Chicago, Illinois; and Elaine, Arkansas.

Elaine, Arkansas

A group of Black men and women met at a small local church in Elaine, Arkansas, on the evening of September 30, 1919. They were sharecroppers, and unlike Clara Belle Drisdale and her family, many of these tenant farmers were exploited by the owners of the land they worked. Greedy landowners did the accounting, deciding how much their tenants' harvests were worth and what the size of their debt was. The law let them demand excessive profits and left sharecroppers with no recourse.

In some areas, the law ordered them to only sell to their landlord at whatever price the landlord chose. Sharecroppers in those places could not legally set up a roadside stand or take their crops to any market except the landlord, even if they could earn more money by doing so. Plus, one bad harvest could increase their debts, sending them into a nearly unbeatable downward spiral.

Laws also prevented you from leaving if you owed money; you had to work for the landowner until your debt was paid. The accounting of that debt was all in the hands of the landowners. "There was very little recourse for African American tenant farmers against this exploitation; instead there was an unwritten law that no African American could leave the farm until his or her debt was paid off."

If the landowner said you owed, you owed. You couldn't even decide to stop farming or leave without risking being beaten or arrested for vagrancy. Or both. Arrest meant being forced into unpaid labor for the duration of your sentence. Virtually every former Confederate state passed strict vagrancy and labor contract laws, as well as so-called anti-enticement measures designed to punish anyone who offered higher wages to a Black laborer already under contract. Black people who broke labor contracts were subject to arrest, beating, and forced labor. Worst of all, their debt was inherited by their children, forcing their children to repeat the same cycle. Apprenticeship laws forced many minors (either orphans or those whose parents were deemed unable to support them by a judge) into unpaid labor for white planters.

Sometimes, escaping that dizzying merry-go-round of hard work and forever-increasing debt meant sneaking away from their homes in secret, becoming refugees and joining the Great Migration of rural Blacks heading to the north and east in search of employment in industrial centers and at least a hope of safety. Some families were forced to leave behind any possessions they could not carry.

The people in the church in Elaine wanted a different choice. They planned to join a sharecroppers' and tenant farmers' union—the Progressive Farmers and Household Union of America (PFHUA). The objective of the PFHUA was the same as that of any union, to improve the lives of its members. Black farmers were not out to pick a fight with landowners. They organized to obtain legal assistance in obtaining their rights. They had hired a white attorney, Ulysses Bratton, to try to get a fair share of their labor and an accurate accounting of their debt. Organizing was a risk, but some of the leaders were war veterans who found the risk acceptable.

A car filled with white men arrived at the church. Someone from the car shot into the building. Some of the men inside the church shot back, and one white man was killed.

That began the Elaine Massacre, the worst of the anti-Black riots that occurred during the Red Summer of 1919. Whites charged that the union was simply a cover for a secret conspiracy to rise up and overthrow white planters, take their land, and rape their women. The sheriff sent out a call for men to help him "hunt Mr. N***** in his lair." More than five hundred armed white people—mostly from surrounding Arkansas counties and Mississippi—jumped into trains, trucks, and cars to answer the call. They fired at every Black person they saw, calling it target practice.

The governor of Arkansas obtained permission from the Department of War to send in hundreds of troops. They were "under order to shoot to kill any negro who refused to surrender immediately." The soldiers worked with vigilantes to kill at least two hundred Black Americans over the next few days. The violence claimed many people who had nothing to do with anything, including four Johnston brothers returning from a hunting trip with no idea what was happening.

Dr. Lewis Harrison Johnston was a physician, surgeon, and wealthy businessman who lived and practiced in Oklahoma. He had returned to Arkansas for a visit with his family. He was a graduate of Meharry Medical College (the same medical school Dr. Aaron Nixon had attended), a member of the National Negro Business League, and of the State Medical, Dental and Pharmaceutical Association of Oklahoma. His wife had died the year before, leaving him the single parent of two children.

The three Johnston brothers with him were David Augustine Elihue Johnston, a dentist, inventor, and member of the National Negro Business League; and Gibson Allen Johnston and Leroy Johnston, who had both recently been discharged from the army. Leroy had served as a bugler in the Harlem Hellfighters. After being wounded in the trenches and gassed during the Battle of Château-Thierry, he spent nine months recovering in a hospital. He received the Croix de Guerre, and later, a Purple Heart posthumously in 2018. Then he came back to the States, where he and three of his brothers were dragged from a train, tortured, and massacred on the way home from a simple family reunion and hunting trip.

A seven-man committee formed to investigate the riot issued a statement declaring the actions, starting with the gathering at the church in Elaine, had been a "deliberately planned insurrection of the negroes against the whites." No evidence was ever produced to substantiate the insurrection claim.

No one was ever arrested or tried for the hundreds of Black lives taken at Elaine. Five whites died. For those deaths, someone had to be held accountable. Twelve of the mob's surviving victims faced hastily convened murder trials. The verdicts were inevitable;

jury deliberations lasted just moments before they handed out the death penalty. NAACP lawyers worked for years to get those sentences overturned. In 1923, the Supreme Court did so. Chief Justice Oliver Wendell Holmes wrote the majority opinion. He stated that "counsel, jury and judge were swept to the fatal end by an irresistible wave of public passion," and the Supreme Court had a duty to guarantee the defendents constitutional rights since Arkansas had failed to do so.

Committee members congratulated themselves for restoring order. They also claimed that not one slain Black was innocent, ignoring the death of children during the riots.

Chicago

The Red Summer arrived in Chicago on Sunday, July 27, on a day when the temperature climbed to 96 degrees Fahrenheit. Tensions ran high in the stifling air. The city had recently experienced several bombings of Black residents. The police had not solved any of them by the day Eugene Williams, a Black teenager, took a make-shift raft to the beach.

Invisible color lines ran through Chicago; there were places where Blacks were not allowed. While the seventeen-year-old played in the cool waters, he unknowingly drifted across one of those lines. A white man threw stones at him for invading the white section of the water, knocking the teen into the lake, where he drowned.

The next night, groups of white men and boys gathered into mobs. They climbed into their cars and invaded Chicago's South Side, where Black residents lived. Many immigrants who feared the continued influx of Blacks into the city would cost them jobs joined in shooting at Black people, burning and looting homes. Most violent incidents during the Red Summer were initiated by ordinary white civilians who were not affiliated with the Ku Klux Klan or any other racist organization. Groups of Black veterans grabbed their guns and formed into militias to confront the rioters and protect Black lives.

The majority were from the Illinois National

Neighborhood children raiding an African American family's house after they were forced out during the 1919 Chicago Race Riots.

Guard's 8th Infantry Regiment. Like the Harlem Hellfighters, they fought with the French during the war since no US general wanted them any more than they had wanted the Hellfighters. Renamed the 370th Infantry, they earned their own nickname from their German enemies: Schwarze Teufel, or Black Devils. The words of a popular World War I song went, *How ya gonna keep 'em down on the farm after they've seen Paree?* In the case of these veterans, the words could have been, *How do you keep Blacks subservient after they've fought for democracy?*

The unexpected armed resistance made the white mob back down, but not before twenty-three Black and fifteen white people were killed and a thousand Black families were left homeless. No white participants in the riot faced any legal consequences.

WASHINGTON, DC

Trouble began in the nation's capital after the white wife of one of the navy's aviation department employees

Couple moving personal belongings in a cart, accompanied by a policeman, during the race riots in Chicago, Illinois, 1919.

claimed two Black men collided with her and tried to steal her umbrella. That tale grew taller with each retelling, until stories filled with marauding gangs of Black rapists spread across the city. "SCREAMS SAVE GIRL FROM 2 NEGRO THUGS," read the headline in the *Washington Times*. The *Washington Post* contributed, "NEGROES ATTACK GIRL, WHITE MEN VAINLY PURSUE." The stories went viral, long before the internet was even a dream, and newswires picked up the words and sent them racing around the country.

Word that a Black suspect had been questioned and released sent white crowds scrambling to grab pipes, clubs, sticks, and pistols. They began a days-long drunken rampage, assaulting, and in some cases lynching, Black people on the capital's streets. The rampage continued around the White House, the Department of War, and even at the Peace Monument in front of the Capitol. They hit predominantly Black neighborhoods and random streets where unfortunate souls found themselves.

Carter G. Woodson, a Howard University professor, Harvard graduate, and one of Washington's leading Black citizens, recalled hearing "a Negro yelling for mercy." He ducked into an entryway to hide from that mob, only to encounter a second mob shortly afterward.

> *They had caught a Negro and deliberately held*
> *him as one would a beef for slaughter, and when*
> *they had conveniently adjusted him for lynching,*
> *they shot him. I heard him groaning in his*
> *struggle as I hurried away as fast*
> *as I could without running, expecting every*
> *moment to be lynched myself.*

A story in the September 1919 issue of *The Crisis*, the official publication of the NAACP, held another eyewitness account from James Weldon Johnson. Johnson was a lawyer, school principal, novelist, poet, and the lyricist of "Lift Every Voice and Sing," known as the Negro national anthem.

I knew it to be true, but it was almost an impossibility for me to realize as a truth, that men and women of my race were being mobbed, chased, dragged from street cars, beaten and killed within the shadow of the dome of the Capitol, at the very front door of the White House.

Law enforcement failed to stop the anti-Black violence. Historian Lloyd Abernathy wrote, "Sensing the failure of the police, the mob became even more contemptuous of authority."

DC's Black veterans grabbed weapons they had brought back from France and stepped in to present a strong, organized resistance. Many of these men had been members of the 1st Separate Regiment, District of Columbia National Guard, another group of Black fighters rejected by US generals. During the war, they were renamed the 372nd Infantry and assigned to serve under French general Mariano Francisco Julio Goybet in the 157th Infantry Division, also known as the Red Hand Division. General Goybet had no problem with

Black soldiers, seeing them only as Americans, "the sons of the soldiers of George Washington who have come over to fight as in 1776, in a new and greater war of independence." They received numerous citations, including the Croix de Guerre and Legion of Honour. By the end of 1918, he told the Black veterans, "To those who ask where you come from, you will answer with pride, 'We are the soldiers of the Division Goybet, the Division with the Red Hand: it was a fine Division!'" Even today, the 372nd Military Police Battalion of the DC National Guard includes a red hand as part of their crest, along with the words "We guard the peace."

Men stationed themselves on rooftops, prepared to act as snipers to protect their neighborhoods. Others set up blockades to protect Howard University. A mob on Seventh and Florida Avenue NW was met by a force of more than a hundred Blacks who dispersed the group.

The police considered attempts at self-defense an uprising. Gun dealers and hardware stores that sold secondhand pistols along with knives obeyed orders not to sell to Blacks. Law enforcement then ordered Blacks to surrender weapons they needed to defend themselves. They refused, feeling that the police, who could not protect them, had no right to order them to commit suicide.

It may seem difficult to believe, but many white people in DC were truly astonished that Blacks dared to defy their orders and fight back. The *New York Times* lamented, "There had been no trouble with the Negro before the war when most admitted the superiority of the white race."

Apparently, "most" Blacks admitted no such thing. That was revealed by a letter in *The Crisis* by someone who identified herself simply as a "Southern Black Woman."

> *The Washington riot gave me a thrill that comes once in a lifetime . . . at last our men had stood up like men . . . I stood up alone in my room . . . and exclaimed aloud, "Oh I thank God, thank God." The pent up horror, grief and*

humiliation of a lifetime—half a century—was
being stripped from me.

The NAACP asked Congress to investigate the riot and DC's justice system. Congressional committees controlled by Southerners blocked the effort. Without an investigation, the only aftermath was the death and destruction in Black areas. The riot dropped out of the news. Gone, but not forgotten. At least not by men like Jasper Williams.

As president of the El Paso NAACP, he could not forget about the hundreds of men, women, and children killed in the riots. Nor could he ignore the eighty-three people who were lynched in 1919, up from sixty-four in 1918. One of those men died locally, in Longview, Texas. Not only did Longview citizens lynch a young Black man named Lemuel Walters, they then beat a teacher and set his home on fire after rumors spread that he was the author of what many white citizens considered an offensive article about the murder for the *Chicago Defender*.

The El Paso NAACP joined the main organization in adopting a more activist platform. That included supporting H.R. 11279, the anti-lynching bill first introduced by Congressman Leonidas Dyer of Missouri in 1918. Although the Dyer bill passed in the House of Representatives, it was killed by a Senate filibuster, sending it to join a long list of failed anti-lynching legislation.

British men picket with anti-lynching placards on behalf of the NAACP.

STARTING A NEW LIFE

Jasper Williams and the NAACP soon faced another struggle, this one involving the right to vote. On May 23, 1923, the Texas state government passed a Jim Crow law disenfranchising—stealing the right to vote from—its Black citizens. Jim Crow was a popular name for state and local laws that stripped essential rights from Black people, turning them into second-class citizens. Some were enacted into official law in the late nineteenth and early twentieth centuries by white legislatures; others were simply customs everyone knew and had to obey.

This particular law stated that "in no event shall a Negro be eligible to participate in a Democratic primary election." At that time in history, Texas was practically a one-party state. A win in the Democratic primary election virtually assured victory in the general election.

Although Dr. Nixon had the receipt to show he had paid his poll tax, he was turned away from a polling place when he tried to vote. As the first president of the El Paso branch of the NAACP, Jasper Williams helped his friend sue the state of Texas. The case became known as *Nixon v. Herndon*. In 1927, the United States Supreme Court, America's highest legal body, unanimously ruled in favor of Dr. Nixon, saying he had been unlawfully deprived of his rights, in clear violation of the Fourteenth and Fifteenth Amendments to the United States Constitution.

Yet that ruling was not enough to force Texas to grant its Black citizens their right to vote. For decades, Texans continued to use legal loopholes to ignore the Supreme Court decision. The court fights lasted until a second Supreme Court ruling on July 22, 1944. Twenty years after he was first turned away, Dr. Nixon walked up to his El Paso voting place and submitted his ballot for the Democratic primary.

The Williams family was no longer in Texas to see that success. Not long after the original lawsuit was filed, a fire destroyed the family drugstore. Jasper and Clara Belle might have chosen to remain in El Paso, but they had three small children to worry about. The youngest, Charles, was a toddler. They packed up the family and left El Paso for Las Cruces, a fast-growing area in the state of New Mexico.

New Mexico is known as the Land of Enchantment, or Tierra del Encanto in Spanish. JB and his brothers found themselves living on the edge of the biologically diverse Chihuahuan Desert, where rain was a special event. Long-eared jackrabbits loped among the desert grasses and creosote bush, with golden eagles soaring above to chase them. Roadrunners raced lizards in the desert scrub, and black-tailed prairie dogs poked their heads above the ground. The Organ mountain range dominated the horizon with peaks that seemed to brush the sky. Bright sunlight filled the sky almost every day of the year, with cloudless evenings ideal for stargazing. Spring winds were strong and harsh enough to sandblast bare skin. Summer temperatures hung around ninety degrees. Winters almost didn't exist, with only about two inches of snow a year.

The Devil's Backbone, Mesa region of Las Cruces.

Mexican and Anglo traditions and cultures mixed together.

The population of Las Cruces included a small but growing Black middle class composed of business owners, tradesmen, and ranchers. Many resided in a mixed Black and Mexican neighborhood near the downtown area. Others ranched and farmed on the land surrounding Las Cruces. The Williams family settled into the integrated neighborhood.

White families from Southern states streamed into Las Cruces. Many were used to enjoying the benefits of Jim Crow laws in their home states. Using a legal principle called "separate but equal," newcomers talked the Las Cruces board of education into segregating the public schools. They did not want their families associating with the area's growing Black middle class—especially not their children. Even white men in Las Cruces who had lived side by side with Blacks for years ended up agreeing that removing "pupils of African descent" from the public schools was best for everyone.

. . . in the opinion of the county school board or municipal school board and on the approval of said opinion by the state board of education, it is for the best advantage and interest of the school that separate rooms [shall] be provided for the teaching of pupils of African descent, and [when] said rooms are so provided, such pupils may not be admitted to school rooms occupied by pupils of Caucasian or other descent. Provided further, that such rooms set aside for the teaching of such pupils of African descent shall be as good and as well kept as those used by pupils of Caucasian or other descent, and teaching therein shall be as efficient. Provided further, that pupils of Caucasian or other descent may not be admitted to the school rooms so provided for those of African descent.

JB and his older brother, Jasper Fleming, were refused admittance to the local public school. Take a moment and imagine how they felt when they were told they didn't belong in the same place as the white and Mexican children who were otherwise just like them. Jasper Fleming once described his memories of those days, with many white people standing around the school saying, "This place isn't for you." Over half a century after the fact, he held his stomach as he admitted, "Something happened inside of me . . . I wanted to go there." His voice still broke, and he struggled to hold back tears before adding, "I said then I will be something, come hell or high water."

The local Black church, Phillips Chapel CME (Christian Methodist Episcopal), provided space to serve as classrooms for the Black elementary and high school students. This allowed the children to continue their education. Clara Belle Williams dusted off her education credentials and took a position teaching elementary school students, including her own sons. The pay was $900 for the school year. The Williams boys found themselves trying to do their lessons in cramped rooms, while the white and Hispanic kids marched into the much larger Central Elementary School building.

A view of the southeast corner of the Phillips Chapel CME church in Las Cruces, New Mexico, following a restoration project begun in 2010.

JB quickly learned he couldn't get away with much, not when his mother was also his teacher. She expected a lot from her students, and even more from her sons. Worse still, his father began working as the principal in the Black high school. This awakened a fear that his high school years would be just as demanding.

Fortunately for him, his father's time as principal didn't last long. Because President Abraham Lincoln had issued the Emancipation Proclamation, which freed the slaves, Jasper Williams decided to give students a holiday on Lincoln's birthday. When the school superintendent objected, the stern, unyielding Jasper told him he could go to "a place that wasn't cold," his wife reported while laughing. The enraged school superintendent not only fired Jasper for that, he had the principal blackballed so he could never work in a New Mexico school again.

Years later, the Williams family discovered that school board records officially listed Jasper Williams as his wife's assistant, not as high school principal! Clara Belle laughed when she listened to the revelation, knowing her hot-tempered husband would never even have taken the job had he realized the records considered him his wife's assistant. "If he had known, he would have quit the next day," she said. Jasper Williams really was full of pride.

After being blackballed from teaching, Jasper purchased 640 acres of land in the windswept mesa area about seven miles east of Las Cruces and started a homestead. He also talked a number of other Black families into buying homesteads.

Jasper turned out to be a good farmer. The family raised vegetables and cotton. He was able to survey a field and tell when the ears of corn would be ready to eat and when melons would be ripe, and he understood how precious water was. He could look at the sky and predict rain. In a land where rainfall was scarce, that ability helped make him one of the area's most successful farmers.

The Williams homestead was a half-day buggy ride from Las Cruces. The boys lived in town during the week to attend school. JB and his older brother, Jasper, spent weekends and summers at the homestead. Charles, born with a birth defect called clubfoot in both legs, stayed in the city with their mother. He had difficulty standing and walking. The tendons around his feet were shorter than they should have been, which left them turned to the side and twisted out of shape. Today, clubfoot can be corrected early in life with casts placed on a newborn's feet. Back in the 1920s, the only treatment was a series of bone-straightening operations that continued through Charles's early years. That meant remaining in the city for frequent doctor visits and hospital treatments.

While Charles read books and attended school year-round, JB and Jasper enjoyed their time spent living wild and free on the family homestead. In many ways, the Williams boys lived a dream life. They had a dog, rode horses, and even drove the family's old John Deere tractor. During the day, the sky was blue as the blueberries in their mother's pies. In the evenings, they gathered wood for fuel and used kerosene lamps to provide light for studying. Math was JB's favorite subject.

There were no such things as boy chores and girl chores. All three boys learned to sew and wash clothes, to cook and preserve food, and to clean the house. JB fed livestock, tended the garden, and collected eggs from chickens. He would volunteer for almost any task if it meant he could avoid having to clean the family outhouse!

Seventy-five sixth-grade Black children were crowded into a single small room with one teacher in an old store building near Negro High School in Muskogee, Oklahoma.

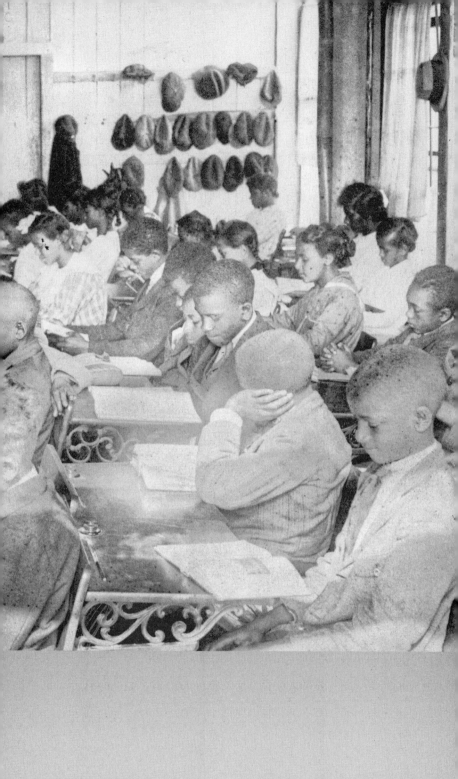

JB couldn't help wondering why white adults seemed to fear having their children get too close to kids like him, kids with brown skin. Being kept separate felt wrong. He watched white students head into the public school building that held new books and supplies and everything else they needed.

Separate, and totally unequal.

SEPARATE BUT EQUAL:
PLESSY V. FERGUSON

SEPARATE BUT EQUAL IS a phrase with a long, ugly history in the United States. It denotes the legal policy regarding racial segregation in the late nineteenth and early twentieth centuries in the US. The policy produced numerous state and local laws that made it legal to segregate Black people from other Americans.

Black and white Southerners mixed relatively freely during the beginning of the Reconstruction period, roughly from the end of the Civil War until 1877. Then came the rise of Jim Crow laws designed to keep Black people "in their place" by removing many of the political and economic gains Black people achieved during Reconstruction, disenfranchising them and taking away jobs and education opportunities. These included vagrancy laws that turned jobless and homeless Black people into criminals, sending many to prison.

"People who never grew up during segregation can't realize how rigid it was," said one Black man. "You could go as high as you could in the Black community, but you couldn't go nearly as high in the white community. Opportunities were denied to you, and you had no recourse. That was why the NAACP and the civil rights movement got started back in the 1920s and 30s."

In addition to laws keeping Black and white children in separate schools, separate but equal separated people in areas such as transportation, jobs, and social situations, including the use of bathrooms and drinking fountains. Black men and women understood the consequences of disobeying both written and unwritten or unspoken rules. In some areas, the penalties included the kind of death Alex Johnson endured back in Cameron. In places called "sundown towns," Black people were not allowed inside town limits after sunset. They might be allowed to work in the towns during daylight hours, primarily as housekeepers, cooks, maids, babysitters, or gardeners, but they were not welcome once their work was done.

White citizens might even be friendly with them during the day. They might wave or call a Black man or woman by name when they passed on the street. At night, that Black person would be attacked, arrested, or even killed for walking the same street. It was almost as if the sight of dark skin was painful to some white people. Maybe it made them uneasy by reminding them of the original sin of slavery. They could only feel comfortable by keeping anyone with dark skin at a distance.

At first, Black people found some freedom from Jim Crow by joining the Great Migration to some of the bigger cities in the North and East, places like Chicago,

"Mississippi at the St. Louis Fair," cartoon by John Tinney McCutcheon.

Detroit, and New York. But Jim Crow spread, too, following them, often making it dangerous for Black people to be anywhere except inside their homes after dark. Defiance of those laws could bring arrest and a long sentence of forced labor.

In the 1880s, the Louisiana state legislature passed a law requiring railroads to place passengers legally described as "people of African descent" in separate railroad cars, away from white men and women. This became known as the Louisiana Separate Car Act.

Like many Southern states, Louisiana law included a so-called one-drop rule. That rule classified anyone with even a tiny drop of African blood in their family tree as legally "Colored," no matter how distant that ancestor or how the person looked. The Louisiana state law codifying the one-drop rule was not repealed until 1983.

Good thing they didn't have DNA testing back then. A lot of very prejudiced white people who believed they had 100 percent European heritage might have been surprised by the results. Over the years, a number of Black men and women with pale skin and European features chose to ignore their African ancestors and call themselves white. Don't blame them for desiring the many benefits being considered white brought people. Being Black in the white world could get a person hurt, or even killed. Consider what happened to Homer Plessy.

A group of people in New Orleans joined together to fight racial segregation. They called themselves the Citizens' Committee. The Louisiana Separate Car Act was one of the committee's main targets. A thirty-year-old shoemaker named Homer Adolph Plessy volunteered to help them challenge that law. Mr. Plessy hoped to make an impact on society that was larger than simply making its shoes. He was a Louisiana Creole, having a single Black great-grandparent among his seven white great-grandparents of Spanish and French heritage. Today he would be called biracial, or even white based on his appearance. Back then, thanks to the one-drop rule, he was just another man of African descent, i.e., Black.

Homer woke that morning knowing he would be in jail by afternoon. He took his time dressing before heading to the New Orleans railroad station. He purchased a first-class train ticket for Covington, Louisiana. He appeared calmer than he felt when he took an empty seat in the white car and waited for the conductor.

The railroad expected him to be there. Plessy appeared white, so the Citizens' Committee had to alert the railroad for their plan to work. Railroad executives did not like the rules forcing them to waste money on an extra car just for Black passengers. They wanted that law overturned and happily agreed to a plan to make Mr. Plessy a test case. When the conductor ordered him to leave and go to the Black car, Homer refused. He was arrested, taken from the train, and jailed. Step one in the plan to overturn the unjust law was a success. Step two was the trial that found Plessy guilty.

Homer Plessy had expected that to happen. He was guilty, but only of disobeying an unjust law. He and

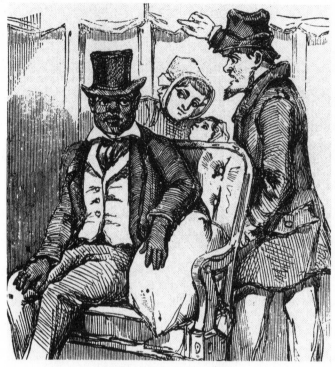

A black man is barred from a railway car in Philadelphia — proof of "Jim Crow" in the North.

Engraving of a white man ordering a Black man to leave a railway car, circa 1850.

the Citizens' Committee had always placed their hopes in the wisdom and justice of the higher courts. They filed suit against the judge, in a case known as *Plessy v. Ferguson*. They based their argument on the Fourteenth

Amendment, which guaranteed all United States citizens equal protection under the law.

When the Louisiana state supreme court refused to see the justice in his cause, Plessy and the Citizens' Committee filed an appeal with the United States Supreme Court. Committee members were certain the nine justices of the highest court of the land would pay attention to the meaning of the United States Constitution.

They were wrong. On May 18, 1896, the conservative majority in the court ruled that Mr. Plessy's rights had not been violated by the Louisiana Separate Car Act. By a vote of eight to one, they said separating whites from Blacks had nothing to do with equal protection under the law. The protections of the Fourteenth Amendment applied only to political and civil rights (like voting and jury service), not social rights (like sitting in the railroad car of your choice).

In addition, the justices blamed Black people themselves for any issues. They said Plessy and others simply assumed that a forced separation of the races stamped Blacks with a badge of inferiority. The problem, the justices insisted, came "solely because the colored race chooses to put that construction upon it."

The high court's decision shook Mr. Plessy and stole his chance to change the world. He didn't choose; he knew. Every Black person in America knew exactly why whites demanded segregation. White newspapers hailed the ruling, which removed any hope Blacks would be allowed the same comfort and convenience as whites. According to an article in the St. Martinville, Louisiana, newspaper, the important thing was that whites would be spared the "discomfort and irritation" of having to share a train car with Blacks.

The Citizens' Committee still believed the law was wrong. However, with nowhere else to appeal, they were disheartened and soon disbanded. The railroad shrugged off its disappointment and solved its financial problem by spending the least amount possible on accommodations for its Black passengers. Their cars were stuffy, cramped, and uncomfortable. Since all passengers arrived at the same stations at the same times, they were also "equal."

Only one of the nine justices disagreed with the majority: Justice John Marshall Harlan, a former slaveholder, who had once opposed emancipation. Over the years he changed his ideas and grew outraged watching the extreme actions of white supremacist groups like the Ku Klux Klan. He predicted the high court's decision would make life worse for Black people.

He was right.

That single ruling made segregated public facilities legal in the United States for the next six decades. The Supreme Court makes decisions based on an interpretation of the US Constitution. Their ruling in this case sent the message to lawmakers and lower courts in Louisiana and all around the country that the Constitution sanctioned segregation laws. *Plessy v. Ferguson* became the basis for many future separate but equal laws, including the one separating the Williams brothers from the white and Hispanic kids in Las Cruces schools. More laws sprang up all over the country barring people with even a drop of African blood among their ancestors from sharing the same buses, schools, hotels, swimming pools, and even hospitals as whites.

Life grew increasingly dangerous for any Black person accused of violating segregation's rules. Both male and female membership in the KKK grew. According to Saje Mathieu, a history professor at the University of Minnesota, "White women were foot soldiers in some of these riots and women 100 years ago were just starting to flex their muscle within the Klan."

GROWING UP JB

JB WAS RIGHT ABOUT one thing. Having Clara Belle Williams as a teacher, and a mother, proved to be an advantage. There was no dillydallying or roaming attention allowed in her class. She saw to it that all her students learned. Her classroom was often hot and dry, and always crowded. The school had no library or gym or science lab, but her wisdom and determination motivated all her students.

Her students included grade-school children like you, whom she taught during the day. In the evenings, she taught adults. Although Clara Belle's father managed to teach himself to read and write, most elderly former slaves had never learned. Now, with their children grown, they finally had time to feed a hunger that had gnawed at them their entire lives. They were learning to read.

If JB ever felt tempted to laugh at their halting efforts, his mother quickly stopped him.

Married, with a full-time job teaching and three growing children, Clara Bell's thirst for knowledge still led her to return to college as a student. She sought a second college degree, this one in English.

She began by taking extension and correspondence courses from the University of Chicago. Then, in 1928, she enrolled for summer classes at the New Mexico College of Agriculture and Mechanic Arts (the school is now called New Mexico State University—NMSU). Because she taught during the regular school year, she could only attend summer school classes, so earning her degree took a long time.

Clara faced a personal struggle with separate but equal rules. The college took her money as tuition for her classes. Then many instructors used the same Jim Crow laws that barred her sons from attending public schools against her. They refused to let her inside their classrooms with their white students. A few left a chair in the hall for her to sit in while she listened to lectures and took notes. Others did not, forcing her to stand during class. In many ways, her determination to succeed made her the embodiment of an old saying: "Until God opens the next door, praise Him in the hallway."

As he grew older, JB spent summers doing yard work for Las Cruces residents to earn money of his own. The largest and grandest homes belonged to well-to-do white physicians. He grew inspired to become a doctor himself, to help people while becoming wealthy and respected. When he shared his plans with his friends, many laughed. His parents cheered him on. They wanted at least one son to become a doctor. They had no idea they would end up with three.

The youngest son, Charles Lee, was the first to decide on a medical career. Charles told his mother,

"I'm going to study medicine and see if I can make all the crippled folks not be crippled anymore."

Life was not all work. The Williams family always had supper, the evening meal, as a family. JB never had a favorite food, although he loved anything with hot chilis. "We were poor, so we had to eat what was available, you know?" he said. Even after he grew up and could afford to eat whatever he wanted, he always ate whatever was on the plate before him.

His parents made certain their boys had time to study and time for well-deserved fun. JB learned to shoot rattlesnakes, loved riding horses, and enjoyed not having to take baths every day. Like many boys and girls, JB often spent time staring up at soaring birds and dreamed of flying over the tops of the mountains. The doctor who picked his little brother up and made sure he got to the hospital for his surgeries happened to be a pilot. JB sometimes watched when the doctor's plane landed in Las Cruces.

At the end of each day, when chores were finished, family members got together and entertained one another. They often made their own music or had fun telling stories—stories that included the exploits of famous people like the outlaw Billy the Kid, who once took refuge in the Organ Mountains. They also told tales of the 9th Cavalry, Black Civil War veterans called Buffalo Soldiers, who were once stationed at nearby Fort Selden. Their main mission had been to secure the road from

The Redoubtable Sergeant, a painting of Buffalo Soldiers, by Don Stivers.

San Antonio to El Paso. They also participated in campaigns against the Apache, Native Americans frustrated with life on reservations and the federal government's string of broken promises. That included participation in what became known as Victorio's War, a conflict between Victorio and the US government.

Victorio was chief of the Chihenne, one of four bands of the Chiricahua Apache tribe living in southwestern New Mexico. One US officer declared that, with the single exception of Crazy Horse of the Sioux, he considered Victorio "the greatest Indian general who ever appeared on the American continent."

Victorio's fight was an attempt to preserve the Apache's right to their sacred land, Ojo Caliente, (Warm Springs). Black soldiers, facing their own forms of discrimination from the federal government, were sent to subdue another minority group in that government's name. In the war, which lasted from 1879 until Victorio's death in 1880, Buffalo Soldiers earned a reputation for courageous service. Many won the Medal of

Honor, an award recogniz-
ing valor that goes above
and beyond the call of duty.

JB also loved hearing
about Elizabeth "Bessie"
Coleman, a Black woman
who wanted to be a pilot.
Her mother was Black, her
father Native American.
When no flight school in
America would agree to
train a Black woman, she

US Army Medal of Honor.

taught herself French, took a second job to raise money,
and headed across the Atlantic Ocean to obtain instruction at the School of Aviation in Le Crotoy, France,
in 1921. She received her license from the Fédération
Aéronautique Internationale, making the young woman
some called "Queen Bess" the first African American
woman and first Native American to hold a pilot's
license. Bessie received a surprising amount of news

coverage when she returned from France to America. That included the white press, which rarely noticed or covered anything in the Black community. Realizing that flying as entertainment could raise money, she made a barnstorming tour of the United States, flying, parachute jumping, and giving lectures to huge crowds. Her star power enabled her to demand that crowds be integrated before she would agree to perform.

Her plans to use the money to build a flying school for other Black Americans ended when she died in a flight accident in 1926. But her example furthered the

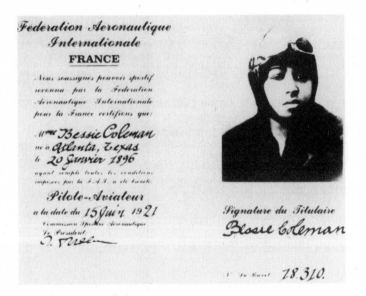

Bessie Coleman's pilot's license.

Bessie Coleman.

dreams of future generations, including the Williams brothers and many future Tuskegee Airmen.

Las Cruces cattlemen hated seeing homesteaders fencing off land they considered theirs. The result was a series of conflicts. They rarely turned violent. Mostly they amounted to inconveniences, like cattlemen cutting the fences so their cattle could enter and graze on the homesteaders' land. But there was one incident JB never forgot.

The Williams family owned a dog named Tony, a little white spitz. Spitzes are companion dogs that were originally bred to be herders, to guard livestock guards, and to hunt. Tony was super protective, as if he fully understood the dangers the times presented to his humans. "He protected us, you know, and nobody could ever touch us, you know?" More than once, JB woke in the darkness to the sound of loud barks. The feisty dog went into action whenever local cattlemen cut the fences around the Williams's homestead to let their cattle graze on the family's land. Tony's upright ears picked up even the faintest sounds. He barked to alert his people, and if you've ever heard a spitz bark, you know no one could ignore that sound. These dogs have oversized vocal cords and love using them.

Tony helped chase cows off the Williams's land while father and sons repaired damaged fences. At least once a week, the dog ran all the way to town to check on Clara Belle while she taught. Once satisfied she was fine, he turned and headed back to the homestead. This continued until his death.

JB was sure he knew how his dog died.

. . . the cattlemen, I'm pretty sure it was

cattlemen that killed him. I can't imagine anybody

else wanting to kill a dog who was . . . all

he was doing was going down the road going home.

Although he was in his nineties when he talked about Tony, his voice filled with tears as he added, "He was a great friend, too."

Clara Belle continued standing in the halls of NMSU, attending classes every summer until 1937. Day after day, summer after summer, JB watched her return home from her studies on tired feet. Sometimes he had to swallow down rage, but her example helped him believe he could do anything, including becoming a doctor.

She became the first person of African descent to receive a degree from the all-white college at the age of fifty-one. Her bachelor's degree was in English, with a minor in mathematics. She never got to walk across a stage to pick up her diploma in front of her family. Her white classmates threatened to boycott the graduation. No one wanted to walk in front of her, or behind her.

As a result, the graduation ceremony was canceled. No students walked across the stage; the graduates had to pick up their degrees from the registrar's office.

Clara Belle Williams admitted that many things in life were not fair, but she never let that stop her. She told her sons, "You can do whatever you want to if you put your mind to it and work hard."

Eldest son Jasper Fleming was the first to take that advice. After graduating from high school, he enrolled at Tuskegee Institute in Alabama. Tuskegee is an HBCU, one of America's Historically Black Colleges and Universities. It was founded by Booker Taliaferro Washington, one of the leading African American intellectuals of the nineteenth century. The son of an unknown white man and an enslaved mother, Booker T. Washington grew to become an educator, author, and advisor to both President Theodore Roosevelt and President William Howard Taft. Jasper studied hard and became an honors student. He earned a bachelor's degree in business administration in 1940 and then returned to Las Cruces to start his own business.

There were only about twenty students in JB's one-room high school. His graduating class included three students. One was a boy who went on to become a chiropractor. The second was a girl who went on to college. JB was the third. He enrolled at NMSU and studied biochemistry as his first step toward becoming a doctor. Like his mother before him, he had to work his way through college.

You might ask why JB decided to enroll in the same school that had mistreated his mother. Perhaps he felt defiant, or experienced a desire to walk in her footsteps. Or maybe he just wanted to remain close to home after seeing his older brother go to school so far away. At least one thing had changed for the better. After his mother cracked the color barrier, instructors at the formerly all-white college allowed him to sit inside classrooms and labs with the other students. He studied hard, worked hard, and did well. Even though a shortage in finances forced him to take some time off in the middle of his studies and work full-time, life and the future looked good.

Then the United States entered World War II.

DOUBLE V FOR VICTORY

IN THE EARLY MORNING hours of December 7, 1941, the Japanese launched a surprise attack on the US naval base at Pearl Harbor on Oahu, Hawaii, plunging the United States into World War II. Although Black men rushed to volunteer for the fight, white soldiers once again refused to perform combat duty alongside them. Generals allowed this and maintained that forcing integration on white soldiers would diminish their effectiveness.

At the start of World War II, it appeared Black volunteers and draftees would face the same losing game they had to play in World War I. Segregation was the order of the day in most parts of the armed forces. Bases had separate blood banks, hospitals or wards, medical staff, barracks, and recreational facilities for Black soldiers. White soldiers and local white residents routinely insulted and harassed Black servicemen. Yet, once again, Blacks begged for the right to fight on the front lines.

African American leaders, the Black press, and organizations like the NAACP were determined this time things would be different. They advocated for Black fighting units by pointing out the hypocrisy of fighting another war that was theoretically about democracy while at the same time having a racially segregated army.

Military commanders countered, saying the army was no place for a social experiment like integration. They continued to insist that mixing the races would destroy the fighting effectiveness of white soldiers and pointed to that 1925 Army War College report as proof. The accomplishments of Black soldiers like the Buffalo Soldiers and Harlem Hellfighters were shoved aside. The few Black military officers such as recently promoted Brigadier General Benjamin O. Davis Sr. were ignored. He began his military career as a Buffalo Soldier after lying about his age so he could enlist at sixteen without his parents' permission. He rose through the ranks through sheer skill and determination. Maybe he was easy to forget because the army twisted into a pretzel to keep him out of any position where he might command white men and left him in the role of professor of military science and tactics at an HBCU.

Influential Black leaders increased the pressure on President Franklin Delano Roosevelt to let Black soldiers show what they could do with weapons instead of shovels or cooking pots. Jasper Williams was not among them. He wasn't sure Black men should fight and die for a country that still refused to pass a federal anti-lynching law and feared his sons would be sent to fight. Others kept up the pressure until the president agreed to create all-Black fighting units.

Jasper Fleming Williams was the first of the Williams boys to be drafted. The army placed him in an all-Black fighting unit. They would be going over-seas, no ditchdigging or serving as a cook involved. Some of them would die.

Private Jasper Williams attended Fort Bragg for basic training as a field artilleryman. His regiment, like almost every other segregated fighting unit, was commanded by white officers. During training, he put his athletic prowess on display and became bantam-weight boxing champion for his battalion. He went on to become a semifinalist at a regimental tourna-ment. Every time Jasper was knocked down, he jumped back into the fight. His commanding general grew so impressed by his willingness to keep getting up that he was promoted to the rank of corporal and transferred to the officer candidate group.

The Field Artillery Officer Candidate School (OCS) was nicknamed the ninety-day-wonder school. The OCS was started in 1941 when the Department of War realized they needed a faster way to commis-sion officers. Successful students earned a commission as a second lieutenant. OCS was tough, with classes requiring mental agility and physical strength. Students even had to learn the right way to bark orders. At one point during World War II there were ten different OCS schools: Armor, Cavalry, Coastal Artillary, Field Artillery, Engineering, Infantry, Medical Corps, Ordnance, Quartermaster, and Signal Corps. In the years since the end of World War II, when the Department of War became the Department of Defense, there have been changes to the OCS. Sometimes schools have been combined, at other times new groups added, based on the changing needs of the military. Today there are five Officer Training Schools, one each for the Army, Marine Corps, Navy, Coast Guard, and Air Force.

OCS training classes were not segregated. There were relatively few Black students, and the men experienced almost no problems with shared facilities. Years after the war, one Black OCS graduate described the experience by saying, "Inside OCS we were integrated. Accommodations, sleeping, eating, everything, integrated. One foot outside that area, you're back to segregation."

While some instructors were prejudiced and eager to wash out non-whites, most of the training was even-handed. Efforts were designed to produce candidates tough enough to succeed, regardless of skin color. Clara Belle Williams's eldest son did well in that environment. Jasper not only graduated and received his commission as second lieutenant, he earned a spot in the Fort Sill Artillery OCS Hall of Fame. He went on to see service in France and Germany, earning a promotion to lieutenant and two battle stars before the war ended.

Knowing it was likely he, too, would be drafted soon, JB devoured newspaper stories about the war. Black newspapers like the *Pittsburgh Courier* carried stories the white mainstream news often ignored. One day in 1942, a letter to the editor from a Black man named James G. Thompson grabbed JB's attention. Mr. Thompson asked important questions:

> *Being an American of dark complexion and some*
> *26 years old, these questions flash through my*

mind: Should I sacrifice my life to live half-American? Would it be too much to demand full citizenship rights in exchange for the sacrificing of my life?

JB echoed those questions. His father remained totally against the war, still unwilling to have his sons going overseas to fight for a country that would not even pass a federal law outlawing lynching. JB understood his father's reasons. Nevertheless, he knew that if called to serve, he, too, would fight to defend the United States, even if the result was his own death. He agreed with the way Mr. Thompson ended his letter.

There is no doubt that this country is worth defending . . . Let me say that I love America, and am willing to die for the America I know will someday become a reality.

That letter said what many Black Americans felt. It sparked the Double V Campaign in minority communities. V for victory over Hitler in the war abroad, *and* V for victory against the discrimination and racial segregation still filling American society and the military. The slogan was used by Black journalists and activists to rally support for equality. The campaign highlighted the contributions the soldiers made in the war effort.

JB's turn to serve his country came later in 1942. Because of his experience as a premed student, the army assigned him to the medical corps and sent him to Camp Pickett in Virginia. There he worked in the post hospital, caring for sick and wounded soldiers returned from the battlefield. Segregation remained the rule, Black and white members of the medical corps lived in separate barracks. Blacks were forced to use separate facilities: a separate cafeteria, a separate chapel, even a separate movie theater.

In the darkness of that theater, JB watched newsreels covering the war. He hoped for news of his brother's infantry regiment, but the exploits of Blacks were seldom featured. The Office of War Information (OWI)

The Ink Spots, including James G. Thompson, Doc Wheeler, and Ken Bryan, holding sheet music for "A Yankee Doodle Tan," flash the V for Victory sign, for the Double V Campaign, in Pittsburgh, Pennsylvania, 1942.

sent out "black interest" footage to a small firm that catered to Black movie houses, a procedure that kept material featuring Black GIs out of general circulation. The Tuskegee Airmen were an exception. JB got to see Black Army Air Corps officers earning awards for victories against the enemy in the air. Watching them engage in dangerous dogfights (plane-on-plane battles) on the screen brought back his long-ago dreams of flying.

JB was smart and strong, and took on every job hospital employees asked him to perform. His premed training helped him provide exceptional care to patients. He performed his assignments so well his superiors recommended him for a promotion. They proposed sending him to the army's Medical Administrative Officers Candidate School (Medical OCS). After graduation, as a new second lieutenant, he would have been assigned to provide medical support for a fighting unit. While the experience and training would have been a great next step for a future doctor, he had other ideas.

Deep inside, James Buchanan Williams remained the boy who stared up at birds with envy and dreamed of soaring through clouds like Bessie Coleman. While waiting to be drafted back in New Mexico, he had even enrolled in a night class studying airplane engines. Yes, he intended to become a doctor once the war ended. Right now, he saw an opportunity to fly!

He decided to take charge of his own future, and took an unauthorized trip to the recently constructed Pentagon, located only about 150 miles away from Camp Pickett. There he met with the major in charge of procurement and requested to be transferred to the Army Air Force instead of Medical OCS. The major agreed and promised to transfer him within three weeks, proving that sometimes you only have to ask to get what you want.

JB expected to head to Tuskegee Institute for flight training. Instead, his transfer orders sent him on an around-the-country training expedition that began in Boca Raton, Florida. That's where the army conducted B-25 training in armament, communications, and engineering for the future 477th Bombardment Group. The 477th would be the first regiment of Black bombardiers.

After three months as an aviation cadet in Boca Raton, JB was sent to Yale University in New Haven, Connecticut, for six months of technical training. He studied with about 15,000 other cadets. Twenty-six of them were Black, and all were smart and capable. His Black classmates proved that after the war, when four went on to earn PhDs (doctor of philosophy degrees), one became president of a college, another an MD. By the time he left Yale, JB had his commission as a second lieutenant engineering officer. After that he was briefly stationed in New Jersey, where B-25 engines were built, and California, where the planes were manufactured.

His final stop was Colorado for some on-the-job flight training. He flew as copilot in a B-25 bomber. During this period, he was the only Black man in the group. By the time he joined the 477th at Selfridge Field near Detroit, Michigan, he was a twenty-five-year-old first lieutenant and engineering officer. He was also a Tuskegee Airman. No matter where they trained, all Black World War II aviators were Tuskegee Airmen.

ELEANOR ROOSEVELT

LET'S STOP AND TAKE a step backward in time. At the beginning of World War II, JB's dream of flying for his country would have been impossible. Even after President Roosevelt agreed to create Black infantry troops and Jasper Fleming was sent to Europe to fight, the Army Air Corps, the branch of the military that eventually became today's Air Force, continued to resist the idea of Black aviators. Pilots, navigators, and engineers were all officers. General Henry Arnold, chief of the Army Air Corps, refused the idea of Negro pilots "since this would result in having Negro officers serving over white enlisted men. This would create an impossible social problem."

That is why no Black man was admitted to any Army Air Corps classes—not even the son of Colonel Benjamin Davis Sr., who became the first Black man to graduate from the army academy at West Point in the twentieth century. The First Lady, Eleanor Roosevelt, played a major role in changing the color of the war in the air.

Eleanor's life was almost the exact opposite of JB's. She was born into wealth in the big-city bustle of 1890s New York. He grew up with a loving and supportive family. Her parents had marital problems, and her mother considered Eleanor's appearance a disappointment. Her mother died when she was eight, her father when she was ten. The awkward, serious orphan lived with her grandmother until the age of fifteen. Then she traveled to a finishing school in England. Finishing school was a fancy name for a boarding school that specialized in preparing young girls to become good society wives. The school focused on etiquette, the social graces, and upper-class cultural rites. Fortunately, she met a teacher with relatively radical ideas, who promoted social responsibility and independence for young women. Eleanor became actively involved in social reform.

Somewhere in the middle of all the turmoil in her life, Eleanor learned to care about others. She returned to the United States at eighteen, filled with concern for women's issues and civil rights. At twenty, she married her cousin Franklin Delano Roosevelt. (Before you ask, they were fifth cousins.) Her concern for others did not change when she married, not even when her husband contracted an illness called polio that left him paralyzed from the waist down in 1920, a year after their wedding.

She became First Lady in 1933. At that time, America lay trapped in the middle of the Great Depression. All over the country, people stood in bread lines and begged for work. Bored by the role of political wife, Eleanor plunged into her favorite issues: child welfare, housing reform, and equal rights for women and minorities. Being First Lady gave Eleanor one of those "bully pulpits" her uncle Theodore Roosevelt, the twenty-sixth president, had spoken about during his presidency. He used the word *bully* as an adjective meaning "excellent" or "first rate." Her position meant people listened to her.

Eleanor traveled around the country, serving as the president's eyes and ears. That role enabled her to promote her causes and share her thoughts and actions with the world. You can think of her as an early-twentieth-century "podcaster" and "influencer." She wrote a syndicated daily newspaper column called "My Day" that had followers all over the country. She also had a monthly magazine column and hosted a weekly radio show.

Mrs. Roosevelt lobbied her husband unsuccessfully to make lynching a federal crime. He was too worried about losing support from Southern states to agree. She was more successful when she joined the NAACP and worked with African American leaders, trying to ensure Black soldiers had a meaningful role in the war effort. She was so successful that some of her enemies, including J. Edgar Hoover, the director of the Federal Bureau of Investigation (FBI), began spreading the rumor that she was of mixed race. She used her "My Day" column to respond to the questions and rumors, saying, "none of us know how much nor what kind of blood we have in our veins, since chemically it is all the same."

After convincing the president to set up Black infantry units for the ground war, she went after the air.

The very determined First Lady Eleanor decided to combat the negative ideas about Black pilots with a trip to Tuskegee, Alabama. Prior to the start of World War II, Tuskegee Institute was one of five HBCUs that hosted a government-sponsored Civilian Pilot Training Program (CPTP) specifically for Black college students. She looked over the airfield, found the instructors and flight students impressive, and decided she wanted a ride.

At the age of three, Eleanor had been involved in an accident when two ships collided at sea. She and her parents had to be evacuated in a lifeboat. Although she usually appeared forceful and fearless, boats and the sea terrified her after that. But she had no problem with the air. She insisted on taking a flight in a two-seater Piper Cub aircraft with Chief Anderson, one of the Black instructors.

Charles Alfred "Chief" Anderson Sr. couldn't remember a day in his life when he didn't want to fly. When he was young, he saved his money and bought an airplane even though he couldn't find anyone willing to teach him how to operate his plane. He was young and determined. Some people teach themselves how to drive; he decided to teach himself to fly.

There was no internet back then. He had no YouTube instruction videos to help. At first, all he could do was taxi back and forth on the ground. He attended an aviation ground school, hung around airports, and picked up information from white pilots whenever he could. The day came when he decided he knew enough. After taxiing, he took off, soaring into the sky. Fortunately, he was able to land safely, too.

Anderson continued studying and eventually became the first Black American to earn a commercial pilot's license. During his lifetime, he taught thousands of students and became known as the father of Black aviation. His commercial license meant he could fly passengers, including the First Lady of the United States.

Members of her Secret Service detail grew apoplectic. They had already warned Chief Anderson not to fly her around, but when she asked, he decided she was the boss. Her agents frantically called the White House hoping for an excuse to stop her from climbing into Chief Anderson's plane. But when Eleanor Roosevelt made up her mind on something, there was no stopping her. She even insisted that her flight with Anderson be photographed.

The chief kept her in the air for over thirty minutes. After her flight, the First Lady became a strong supporter of the flight program at Tuskegee. She wrote a glowing description of her flight experience in her "My Day" newspaper column. Photographs of Chief

Anderson with Mrs. Roosevelt in the plane circulated across the country. All this helped shut down the myth that Blacks were not capable of flying airplanes. In fact, for millions of Americans, her account of that flight was the first time they were even aware of any Black people flying airplanes. She had one special audience member in mind: her husband.

Shortly afterward, the president agreed that Black men deserved a chance to fly for their country. He directed the United States Army Air Force to accept Black aviation cadets. Eleanor wasn't done. She used her influence to help Tuskegee secure a loan they used to bring the airfield up to military standards. With that, Tuskegee was selected as the training home for the first all-Black Army Air Corps unit, the 99th Pursuit Squadron.

First Lady Eleanor Roosevelt with C. Alfred "Chief" Anderson, a pioneering Black aviator and instructor at Tuskegee Institute, in a Piper J-3 Cub trainer.

LIEUTENANT DAVIS

THE BLACK MEN HEADED for the first Army Air Corps class at Tuskegee Airfield recognized this as an opportunity. For Army Air Corps leaders, the Tuskegee program was an experiment, one most believed would fail. But the Air Corps made two major mistakes.

Historians feel the first mistake the Corps made was in assigning Colonel Noel F. Parrish as commandant of cadet training at Tuskegee Airfield and flying school. Despite his Southern roots (Parrish was born in Kentucky), he was willing to give the men a real chance. He was genuinely determined to help them become successful pilots, fully prepared for combat. He believed his job was to train the Black cadets, not fail them.

He succeeded, with most of the aviators in his classes graduating. He was compassionate and firm and worked to promote high morale among the Black cadets. For example, when he realized an unwritten separate but equal policy had one of the restaurants on the base reserved for white officers only, he used his authority to change things. The restaurant was integrated without violence. White officers who clung to segregation and refused to sit and eat with the Black aviators they worked beside stopped going to the place. Everyone else ate together.

Parrish was once asked, with all seriousness, how Blacks could fly. According to former president George W. Bush, Parrish answered the silly question with a quip: "Oh, they fly just like everybody else flies, with stick and rudder." Most of the Black airmen who trained at the Tuskegee Airfield remembered him as a highly respected leader. They described him as tough but fair, a man willing to give everyone an honest chance.

Tuskegee Airmen prepare to receive their commissions and wings from Colonel Frederick V. H. Kimble, commanding officer of the Tuskegee Army Flying School, Tuskegee, Alabama, 1942.

The second mistake Army Air Corps leaders made was in allowing then-lieutenant Benjamin O. Davis Jr. to join the first class at Tuskegee. The son of the first African American to become a general in any branch of the United States military did not know what failure meant.

Benjamin O. Davis Jr. attended high school in Cleveland, Ohio. That's where he first went to classes among white students. They accepted him because of his character and hard work. He was even elected president of his senior class. The young man expected a similar experience after graduation when he entered West Point, the US Military Academy. It must have stung like a swarm of hornets to find out he was wrong. No one there cared about his character or work ethic. All that mattered to his fellow cadets was the color of his skin.

He was the first Black cadet accepted in West Point in the twentieth century. In a race or competition, it feels good to be number one. The first person to climb Mount Everest or to reach the South Pole received honors. First

Brigadier General Benjamin O. Davis Sr. looks on as a Signal Corps crew erects poles, somewhere in France.

20794

Captain Benjamin Oliver Davis Jr. climbs into an Advanced Trainer in Tuskegee, Alabama.

to orbit Earth, land on the moon. Maybe someday you will be the first to travel to another star. These kinds of firsts are groundbreaking and fuel the imagination.

Other types of firsts are no fun. That often happens when being a first also means being an only. Being the only one of your kind is almost never fun, especially when you find yourself completely ostracized, the way Ben Davis Jr. was at the military academy.

No one wanted him there. Not one of his white classmates would talk to him unless they were ordered to. Imagine having no friends. No one to talk to for four years. He never had a roommate and always ate by himself. He was like his father: No matter what the other cadets threw at him or how badly he was treated, he refused to give in. People expected him to give up. Think how strong that young man had to be, both in muscles and in mind, to keep going month after month, year after year, with no one. The silent treatment might have sent some people running, but it only fueled his determination to show his capabilities.

During his third year at West Point, Davis applied to the Army Air Corps but was rejected because they did not take Blacks. Segregation robbed him. It also robbed his fellow students. Although some of his classmates admitted they admired him, they all threw away a possible friendship with a great man and a future general.

In spite of everything people did to make him quit, Davis graduated in 1936 in the top third of his class. He made a vow to fight segregation in the armed forces but had to start his career serving in one of the Buffalo Soldiers infantry regiments. Like his father, Lieutenant Davis was kept away from positions where he might end up in command of white soldiers. Eventually he was assigned to a position his father once held, teaching military science and tactics at Tuskegee University.

The minute President Roosevelt opened the door to pilot training for Black men, Lieutenant Davis grabbed a spot in the first class. He became one of the five men to graduate from that class on March 7, 1942. After graduation, he was promoted to the rank of lieutenant colonel and named commander of the fledgling 99th Pursuit Squadron.

The unit grew with every successive class of Black cadets. Those who finished were the best of the best. They were trained in celestial navigation—that is, using the stars and sextants to find their way just like ancient sailors. They excelled in stretching fuel and flying safely on fumes. Sometimes men returned to

Brigadier General Benjamin O. Davis Sr., Lieutenant Colonel Noel F. Parrish, and Lieutenant Colonel Benjamin O. Davis Jr., during World War II.

base with barely three minutes of flying time left in their gas tanks. They formed a "Three Minute Egg Club," an elite group with membership limited to those forced to land within that narrow margin.

A year after the first class of pilots graduated, there were enough Black pilots to form a squadron. Davis took them to fight in North Africa, determined to show they were the best of the best. A year later, he assumed command of the second unit of Tuskegee Airmen, the 332nd Fighter Group. They went to fight in Italy. The Army Air Corps allowed units to decorate their planes any way they wanted. The 332nd chose to paint the tails of their planes a fiery red. That color scheme made them instantly identifiable and earned them the nickname Red Tails.

Bombers are large planes designed to get close to ground targets and drop bombs to destroy them. The targets often included antiaircraft guns. Enemy fighters attacked bombers in the air, taking advantage of their lack of maneuverability. American fighter planes and bombers were housed at different air force bases in Europe. Fighters were assigned to escort bombers and protect them from enemy fighter attack. Without an escort, nimble enemy planes caused heavy losses to bombers and their crews. Fighters sent to rendezvous with bombers sometimes had to wait for the bombers to arrive and occasionally had to leave the bombers unprotected and return to base when they ran low on fuel. Others would sometimes fly off and engage enemy fighters to score a "kill," which could leave the slower, less maneuverable, and unprotected bombers at the mercy of new enemy planes.

When the 332nd was assigned to escort bombers, that never happened. "Your job, take them in, bring them out," Colonel Davis instructed his men. "Don't go out running around trying to be an ace shooting down enemy airplanes. That's not your job . . . you shoot them down, somebody else will shoot down one of the bombers. Stay with your bombers."

Tuskegee Airmen stayed. They protected even though tradition gave airmen the right to chase down

Pilots of a 15th AAF squadron and members of "The Three Minute Egg Club."

Lieutenant Dempsey W. Morgan, Lieutenant Carrol S. Woods, Lieutenant Robert H. Nelson Jr., Captain Andrew D. Turner, and Lieutenant Clarence P. Lester were pilots with the 332nd Fighter Group. The elite, all-Black fighter group were better known as Tuskegee Airmen.

enemy planes and seek personal glory. They may have chafed at orders that cost them the opportunity to win the title of Ace, but they obeyed. They could not afford to make a mistake, not with so many generals expecting them to fail.

Bomber crews soon learned that Colonel Davis's Red Tails could be depended on to get them home safe. The Red Tails would always wait, even when the bombers were late to a rendezvous point.

Soon, almost every bomber crew wanted a Red Tail escort.

One Tuskegee Airman, Roy Chappell, stated that he ran into former bomber crewmen as late as 2002, who told him, "Man, when the Red Tails would come up there, I would say, 'Thank the Lord,' because I know I'm going to get home tonight." Another man said, "I owe you guys something, 'cause, my old man told me about them Red Tails. That's the only reason I'm here, 'cause my old man got back."

Colonel Davis Jr. flew sixty combat missions himself. Bomber crews began to special request the

Red Tails as their escorts, trusting the Black pilots to keep them safe. In return, the Red Tail pilots felt a growing respect for the bravery of crews who took their larger, slower, less maneuverable planes directly into intense antiaircraft fire to launch their bombs.

Brigadier General Benjamin O. Davis pins the Distinguished Flying Cross on his son, Colonel Benjamin O. Davis Jr.

That seemed to require more courage than their job of playing "duck back and forth" with enemy fighters.

While Davis led the Black pilots fighting in Europe, back in the States, the decision was made to expand the Black pilot program with a brand-new unit. In spite of the success of the first two groups of Tuskegee Airmen, many Army Air Corps commanders were reluctant to have yet another group of Black officers in their midst. When the 477th Bombardier Unit was created to be the first bomber unit staffed by Black crew members, they tried to stop the program.

Although the unit was officially born in June 1943, the official start was delayed until 1944. Several veteran members of the 332nd volunteered for the 477th and a chance to show off their own courage.

BOMBARDIERS

JB RECEIVED A RUDE awakening when he joined the 477th at Selfridge Field in Michigan.

Major General Frank O'Driscoll Hunter provided that wake-up message when he visited the field. The man in charge of training crews and replacement teams for bombardment operations was a confirmed segregationist from Savannah, Georgia. Hunter was very different from Colonel Parrish, the firm but fair training commander at Tuskegee Airfield. Hunter acted as if keeping strict lines of segregation was more important than preparing his men to battle the enemy.

James Williams in uniform.

Apparently, he did not care that he was in the North now and the state of Michigan had a civil rights law. He set about establishing Jim Crow at the base by telling his Black officers that:

> This country is not ready or willing to accept
> a colored officer as the equal of a white one. You
> are not in the Army to advance your race. Your
> prime purpose should be in taking your training
> and fighting for your country and winning the war.
> In that way you can do a deal for both your race
> and your country. As for racial agitators, they shall
> be weeded out and dealt with.

Detroit had a history of racial conflict and riot. As spring approached, fears that unrest in the city might return and spread to the Black soldiers stationed nearby led the army to move the 477th to a new location, Godman Field in Kentucky. JB only needed one look around Godman for his farmer's eyes to spot problems. His home in New Mexico saw barely ten

The 477th Bombardment Group was trained to fly B-25 Mitchell bombers, but the war ended before they saw action.

inches of rain a year, and it hardly ever snowed. Spring in Kentucky was cold and wet. Strong rains frequently grounded the B-25s, delaying flight training.

The location posed more difficulties than poor weather. The base might have been great for training pilots on smaller aircraft, such as one-man fighter planes. But the small field was horrible for bombers. A

B-25 was almost fifty-three feet long, with a wingspan of over sixty-seven feet. In comparison, a professional basketball court is only fifty feet wide. B-25s carried a six-man crew that included a pilot, copilot, navigator, bombardier, and two gunners.

As you can imagine, planes that size require long runways, much longer than fighter planes carrying a solitary pilot. Bombers also need a lot of apron space for parking, refueling, and maintenance. The gunnery range at Godman Field was so short it created difficulties for the crews during precision and demolition bombing exercises.

One more problem plagued the bombardment group: racial tension. White officers served as trainers for the Black aviators. They also occupied every important squadron, group, and staff position for captains and above. JB held the rank of first lieutenant. That was the highest rank any Black aviation officer in the 477th was able to achieve outside of positions like chaplain or doctor. Even veterans from the 332nd who had been promised promotions before they transferred were consistently passed over for advancement. Every time a command opening arose, leadership brought in a new white officer to fill the position. Many of the newcomers had fewer flying hours in the B-25 than the competent, proud, and highly qualified veterans they supposedly trained. This inequity added fuel to an increasingly volatile situation.

The army had rules forbidding segregation when it came to officers. According to Army Regulation (AR) 210-10, all social organizations, including officers' clubs, had to offer full membership to any officers on duty at the post. An officers' club is a place for army officers to relax and socialize without regard to differences in rank. Despite that regulation, segregation remained an unwritten law wherever the 477th was based. In Major General Hunter's own words, "as long as I am in command, there will be no social mixing of white and colored officers."

Although the base commander, Colonel Robert Selway, came from Wyoming instead of the American South, he was a devout segregationist like his superior. He severely restricted the movements of the Black officers under his command.

Many evenings found JB and friends at a table in the officers' club at Godman. The atmosphere in the club was friendly. There was good food and enjoyable music, making it a perfect place to form friendships with fellow officers.

Fellow Black officers.

Never mind what army regulations said about officers' clubs being open to all. In real life, once the men of the 477th were stationed at Godman, white officers in the field's officers' club became as rare as ice storms on the Las Cruces mesa: pretty much nonexistent. Instead of socializing with the Black officers they worked with every day, Godman's white officers used the nearby Fort Knox club, which provided them with guest memberships. That effectively segregated the races.

So many white people appeared to only be happy when they were around others like themselves. The white officers were blind to the fact that the men of the 477th were just like them.

Officers.

FREEMAN FIELD

THE 477TH WAS SUPPOSED to be ready for combat
in the Pacific on July 1, 1945. By March, everyone knew
the problems at Godman Field made that date impossible, even though the group had a near-perfect training
record with very few accidents and zero fatalities. The
army ordered the unit to move again. They were headed
for a place called Freeman Field in Indiana.

The men felt as if they had been training forever.
Everyone wanted to finish training and head for the
battlefield and their chance to defend their country. The name of their new base sounded promising.

Surely things had to be better at a place named Freeman Field.

The move began at the end of March. The 477th included over 400 officers and 2,000 enlisted men. Transferring all of them, plus tons of equipment from Kentucky to Indiana, required spreading things out over several days and multiple train trips. JB was scheduled to leave Godman on April 5 with the last group of men.

On April 4, shortly after the men received word that the 332nd shot down twenty-five enemy planes on March 31 and April 1, they got a second piece of news. This came from Lieutenant William "Wild Bill" Ellis, one of the most senior pilots in the 477th. Ellis had moved to Freeman Field a few days earlier. Now he was back at Godman after Colonel Selway called him an agitator and kicked him out. He explained the situation waiting for them at Freeman.

About 100 white officers were stationed at the field. The arrival of over 400 Black officers placed them in the minority and left many feeling unsettled.

Some threatened violence against the newcomers. One white officer apparently stated, "I killed two of them [Black men] in my hometown, and it wouldn't bother me to do it again."

The men were in a fine place while they were up in the air, where only ability mattered. Discrimination came when they returned to the ground. Citizens in the nearby town of Seymour refused to deal with the men of the 477th. Their wives could not shop in town, and the men "couldn't even get a Coke or a hamburger." Worse, the base commander, Colonel Selway, issued an order officially separating white instructors, whom he called "supervisors," from Black officers, who were all considered "trainees" regardless of their rank and experience.

At least twenty of the men were not trainees in any sense, including the Black chaplain, and the doctors assigned to the 477th, along with decorated combat veterans who had flown missions over North Africa, Italy, and Berlin. Men like Quentin P. Smith, a six-foot-tall man who grew up in East Chicago, Indiana. Willa Smith (no relation), an African American woman and

Quentin P. Smith, ca. 1943, center, with other Honor Graduates, Tuskegee Army Airfield.

pioneer in transcontinental flight, taught him to fly at her flight school on Chicago's southwest side. He was chosen to go down to Tuskegee to teach cadets before volunteering to transfer to bomber duty.

From instructor to "trainee."

Supervisors had the use of the original officers' club. That facility included a bar, tennis court, mini-golf park, and swimming pool. All were off-limits to trainees. Selway chased Freeman's noncommissioned officers, the sergeants and corporals, out of their own club and turned it into an officers' club for the Black officers. That facility had a bar and a piano. The white sergeants now had an actual reason to dislike the Black newcomers. Lieutenant Ellis said the colonel worked hard to keep from saying no Colored allowed, but kept slipping up and talking about the white officers' club. He and others booed, called the place Uncle Tom's Cabin, and refused to enter. No matter what words Colonel Selway used, there was no hiding what he meant.

It was like the segregated Las Cruces school system all over again. As if nothing would ever change. Separate, and not even close to equal. JB and the others simply wanted the rights guaranteed all Americans by law and the rules of the armed services. That included equal amenities, and the freedom to advance based

STEPHEN HOTESSE
32218759
M − 44 − 14

Esteban Hotesse, during his service as part of the Tuskegee Airmen, 1944.

on their abilities. No special treatment, just respect for their dignity.

The men had to wonder what more they had to do to prove themselves. They were preparing to fight and die for their country, the same as any other man on the base, white or Black. Or Dominican, like Second Lieutenant Esteban Hotesse.

Hotesse was born in the town of Moca, in the Dominican Republic. He emigrated to the United States with his parents when he was four, and grew up in New York. He and his wife, who was from Puerto Rico, had two children. Official army records listed his name as Steve. After enlisting as a semiskilled construction worker, Esteban worked his way into the flight training program. His race was classified as Negro because of dark skin that left him as victimized as any other Tuskegee Airman.

Esteban had just as much to lose as any other officer of the 477th. Not one deserved to be rendered invisible because white officers were uncomfortable at the sight of brown skin.

The military works because of a chain of command that is strictly adhered to. In your school, when you have a problem with an assignment, you probably go to your teacher to discuss things. Normally, something similar happens in the military. Requests for assistance flow up the chain of command, just as orders flow down. Superior officers give orders, and the men below them on the chain obey or bear the consequences.

The military chain of command would have JB take a complaint to his superior officer. That man would forward the issue to the base commander. But Colonel Selway, the base commander, *was* the problem. Above him was Major General Hunter, who encouraged Selway. Military rules gave JB no clear path for bypassing one, much less both of them.

He could try fighting his way inside the club and demand to be served. But a fight could leave him hurt and thrown out of the military in disgrace, accomplishing nothing. One of his mother's sayings echoed inside his head: *Never doubt you can change the world*. He could change things; he simply needed a plan. He had to use his brains, not his fists.

Growing up the second of three sons, he often felt lost in the middle. Now he stood in the middle of a group of his fellow officers, feeling neither lost nor uncertain. They were gathered to discuss Wild Bill's information and what they should do when they arrived. This was not just about them. Discrimination hurts every American. Whether it involves train seats, schools, or an officers' club, separate has never really been equal.

The men talked for hours. Second Lieutenant Coleman Young, the man with experience in organizing labor protests, led the way to developing the plan of action. He had worked with union activists and civil rights organizers from the time he graduated high school until he was drafted. His efforts to organize fellow workers on the Ford Motors assembly line left him blackballed from the entire auto industry. He had no college experience. He had received his commission through the Infantry OCS. Sometimes, the

COLEMAN A. YOUNG
O1297128
M-44 458

Coleman Young, during his service in World War II as part of the Tuskegee Airmen, 1944.

discussion grew heated, but in the end, his plan was defined by a simple phrase: Go to the club.

Once they arrived in Freeman, the men would divide into small groups. Each group would attempt to enter the instructors' club and request service. There were to be no acts of violence or any action that would diminish their goal. Groups would continue trying to enter as long as the club remained open.

They realized they would meet resistance and arrest was a very high probability. Not everyone was convinced taking action was a good idea. At times, the discussion grew heated. A senior medical officer was overruled after he tried to convince the men they had to obey the base commander.

The officers risked a great deal by sticking up for their rights. That included their army careers and their hopes for successful futures. They did not feel like they were being heroes. They were simply doing what they had to do, checking to find out if they were true military officers, or just tokens.

MUTINY

THE PROTEST BEGAN THE evening of April 5, 1945, one decade before Rosa Parks refused to give up her seat on a bus in Montgomery, Alabama. In essence, the men intended to stage a peaceful sit-in. Today we would recognize their actions as getting into "good trouble," in the words of the late US congressman John Lewis, who began fighting for civil rights at the age of fifteen.

Once the train arrived at Freeman, someone set up an area where each man was checked over. Their uniforms had to be spotless, pants pressed to a knife edge, brass wings polished, fingernails clean. They were not giving anyone a real reason to refuse to let them enter the club. The evening was cool, but men wiped sweat from their foreheads.

An initial group of three officers headed for the officers' club. They planned to request service, and get arrested. As they went, the men reminded themselves of the mantra they used during hard times while training: *Stay focused—Stick to it—Get it done.*

No one knew that someone had snitched to Colonel Selway. The colonel sent Major White, the officer in charge of the club, and a guard, Lieutenant Rogers, to stop them. All but one of the doors to the club were locked. Music and laughter flowed through the entrance like an invitation. Major White and Lieutenant Rogers barred the way.

Rogers stepped forward and said, "This club isn't for you fellows." He wore his full uniform, complete with a standard army-issue .45-caliber weapon on his hip. His sole responsibility that evening was keeping the Black men from entering the club.

Major White told them, "If you men refuse to leave, I will have to place you under arrest."

"We are not refusing to leave. We would like to know *why* we must leave," the men insisted.

"Let's be frank," Major White told the first group. "The truth of the matter is that colored officers are not allowed in this club." Inside the club, a Black bartender stared in disbelief. Major White took their names, placed them under arrest, and told them to return to their quarters. The men left peaceably as ordered. They had accomplished their goal.

If Major White was ready to pat himself on the back for successfully ending the protest, he was premature. He soon discovered he didn't understand the men or the strength of their resolve. In a short time, another group arrived, forcing him to repeat the procedure. Moments later, yet another group showed up.

Second Lieutenant Roger "Bill" Terry arrived with the last group of men to approach the officers' club that night. Terry was a proud young man who had earned his pilot's wings in February 1945.

A proud and intelligent young man, he had been a scholarship-winning basketball player at UCLA before the war. There he roomed with soon-to-be-famous baseball great Jackie Robinson. He graduated at the age of nineteen.

At the club, Lieutenant Rogers once again gave the message that trainees were not allowed inside. When Terry insisted, asking Rogers how he knew they were trainees, the guard admitted, "Well, to be frank, no n***** can come in."

Those words tore apart Terry's intention to remain calm. He felt as if "we had always been fighting, all the time we were in the army, for equal rights." Now, when Rogers attempted to prevent him from entering, Terry pushed his way past the lieutenant and entered the club. The two men with him followed. Major White took their names and sent them back to their quarters under arrest. At the time, Terry was okay with that; they all expected to be arrested. He only found out later that the charges against him were different from the ones facing the other men.

In all, thirty-six officers were arrested before Major White closed the club for the night. The protest resumed the next evening, April 6. The total number of men arrested grew to sixty-one before Major White closed the club again. The only violence recorded during the two-day protest was a jostling charge Lieutenant Rogers lodged against Second Lieutenant Terry and the two officers with him.

Colonel Selway wanted to court-martial every one of the protesters. Numerous officers of the 477th wrote to the army inspector general requesting an investigation. Their complaint noted the hypocrisy of US racial policies, stating: "The continuance of this policy can hardly be reconciled with the world wide struggle for freedom for which we are asked, and are willing, to lay down our lives."

The army inspector general sent several army legal officers to Freeman to investigate the situation. They concluded the men might have misunderstood Selway's rules. They recommended the colonel drop the charges because of possible confusion. Selway reluctantly agreed. After all, he had never really believed Black men were smart enough to be officers, so it was easy to think they had been confused. He released everyone except Lieutenant Terry and the other two men accused of jostling Lieutenant Rogers when they entered the club.

Selway remained determined to avoid race mixing. He got together with his boss, Major General Hunter, and discussed ways to regain control. Since Colonel Selway truly believed the men of the 477th were too foolish to understand his original order, he came up with the devilish idea of composing a new rule. This one would be simple and impossible for anyone to misunderstand. He could order each Black officer to sign a statement signaling they understood the rules about segregation at the base.

A few days later, Colonel Selway published Base Regulation 85-2, "Assignment of Housing, Messing, and Recreational Facilities." That document was carefully crafted to stand up against the armed forces' official policy, AR 210-10. He assembled every officer of the 477th except the three still under arrest and had his new regulation read to them. Then he ordered the men to sign a statement saying they had read the regulation, understood, and would obey in the future.

At first, not one man agreed to sign. When they were together, the Black officers remembered their mantra and stood strong. Selway then separated them, calling each man into private interviews with their immediate commanding officer, along with several other white officers to serve as witnesses and someone to record the proceedings. Each man was presented with the same ultimatum: Sign the statement and agree to obey in the future, or face the consequences outlined in the 64th Article of War. That article stated that disobeying a superior officer during a time of war could be punished by court-martial and imprisonment or execution. (Note, the Articles of War were replaced by the Uniform Code of Military Justice in 1950.)

It is impossible to know how each and every individual officer reacted. Some must have felt they had no choice, so they gave in and signed. Others drafted their own statements, which included their feelings about the discriminatory order. One wrote that obedience "would have done violence to the conscience of the undersigned; it would have constituted moral conduct less than that required of an officer and a gentleman in the Army of the United States." Another stated: "The undersigned wishes to indicate over his signature his unshakable belief that racial bias is Fascistic, un-American, and directly contrary to the ideals for which he is willing to fight and die."

Other men continued to assert their right to disobey what they considered an unlawful order: 101 men out of more than 400 Black officers refused to sign.

Lieutenant David A. Smith summoned the courage to tell his superior officer he didn't think the order to sign was proper. His superior insisted: "Lieutenant Smith, I'm giving you a direct order. You sign this communication, and that's an order." Even though his commanding officer repeated the command multiple times, he continued to repeat, "No, I'm not gonna sign it." He was fully aware he would be arrested.

Lieutenant Quentin P. Smith described his ordeal in front of his commanding officer by saying, "I didn't have any breath, I didn't have any saliva left to say anything ... I shook my head because I couldn't even talk." The six-foot-tall gentle giant with a booming voice had always been willing to stick his neck out for what was right. Now he had done it again. Confined to his quarters after refusing to sign, he sat, thinking, "This just can't be true. I'm just about 190 miles from home and this just can't be happening."

Segregation was no shock to Flight Officer Hiram Little, a Georgia native. He had grown up surrounded by Jim Crow. But the army was supposed to be different. He had no idea what he would do or say until the moment his commanding officer gave the order to sign. That's when he realized, "If I go up here and sign this thing, I'm gonna say I agree to segregation and I'll be lying to myself and I have to live with that the rest of my life, and I don't want to do that ... I, I, I, I refused to sign."

When his turn came, Lieutenant James Buchanan Williams faced Major John B. Tyson, a man he considered a friend as well as his commanding officer. He had no idea what anyone else had done. Even if every other man had signed on to the racist regulation, he could not. Instead, he reminded the major that the document violated army regulations.

Major Tyson's scowl deepened, almost as if he really knew what he was asking for was inhumane. Still, he insisted and reminded JB that refusing to obey an order in a time of war could be punished by execution.

The air flew from JB's lungs. He was only twenty-six. He risked a great deal by refusing: not just his army career and his hopes for a future in medicine, but perhaps even his life. All he had to do to save himself was to follow orders. Sign a paper agreeing that he, as a Black officer, deserved to be kept separate from his white counterparts.

A thousand thoughts must have flashed through his head. His mother's sore feet when she returned home after standing in the college hall. His father losing his

Tuskegee Airmen Memorial plaque.

job for daring to speak his mind. Former slaves who worked late into the evening to obtain the education they had never been allowed to even hope for before emancipation.

He could not surrender his dignity. The order to do so was not legal. He could not sign, no matter what price he had to pay. "If I don't have the same rights as an officer as you do then I shouldn't be one," he told his commanding officer. The major ordered the guards to take JB back to his barracks.

As they escorted him away at gunpoint, he wondered whether he would be hanged or shot simply for asking that the American military live up to the creed it claimed to be fighting for.

THE 101 CLUB

COLONEL SELWAY APPLIED SO much pressure that more than three-fourths of the men eventually signed. JB, Esteban Hotesse, Coleman Young, Quentin P. Smith, and ninety-seven others continued to refuse. Those men became known as the 101 Club and their act of refusal was known as the Freeman Field Mutiny.

JB soon learned that execution, at least, had been taken off the table. Instead, he and the others faced the possibility of twenty years of imprisonment at the US penitentiary at Leavenworth, Kansas. If convicted, they would be old men before they saw freedom again. That didn't change JB's mind. He would stay in prison forever before admitting his skin color made him less of a man.

The members of the 101 Club, plus three (Lieutenant Terry and the other two officers accused of jostling) were roused in the middle of the night. Guards forced them out of their bunks and onto a series of C-47 transport planes. The C-47 is a twin-engine, propeller-driven plane, the military equivalent of the DC-3 civilian passenger plane. The military affectionately called them "gooney birds" after a seabird known for its endurance.

The planes took JB and the others back to Godman Field. There they were met by guard dogs and military police armed with submachine guns, like enemy prisoners of war. At the same time as the US Army was liberating German concentration camps, the 477th was locked away behind fourteen-foot fences topped with barbed wire and under the harsh glare of klieg lights, searchlights designed to project powerful beams of light, as they awaited court-martial. Sometimes the white soldiers guarding them looked

C-47 transport plane.

like they hoped for an excuse to pull their triggers. German POWs held at Godman walked around the base freely without guards. They mocked the Black Americans over the treatment they received from their own countrymen.

Morale among the members of the 477th left at Freeman plummeted. General Hunter tried to keep the problems secret. But the officers of the 477th

The men of the 101 Club are lined up after their arrest and are about to be loaded on planes for return to Godman Field for courts-martial.

wrote formal complaints through official channels, communicated with organizations like the NAACP, and tipped off a local reporter so that the incidents were documented in the press.

When he was unable to keep word of the arrests from spreading across America, Selway issued a statement to the local paper, the *Seymour Daily Tribune*, claiming he was only following an existing Army Air Corps policy forbidding personnel in training from using the same recreational facilities as the men who trained them.

Many white Hoosiers read the *Seymour Daily Tribune* and agreed with his argument. (*Hoosier* is a friendly nickname for people from the state of Indiana.) Black men and women saw through that excuse and raised an outcry. The soldiers left behind at Freeman contacted friends, relatives, and the NAACP. About 110 officers wrote letters of protest to the army inspector general.

Although cameras were confiscated from the prisoners, one soldier hid a camera in a shoebox and took a picture of the prisoners waiting to board the transports taking them back to Godman. Black newspapers like the *Chicago Defender*, the *Kansas City Call*, and the *Pittsburgh Courier* filled their front pages with stories of how a quarter of the officers of the 477th, including decorated combat veterans, awaited trial. All for disobeying an order designed solely to enforce illegal segregation. They printed the picture of the men lined up in front of the transport with a headline shouting: "These 477th Bombardment Officers Bombard Jim Crow." The *Pittsburgh Courier* called for the immediate release of the members of the 101 Club, stating that "anything less will be a travesty of justice."

The result was a public relations nightmare for the US military. A tidal wave of Americans voiced solidarity with the mutineers. Lawmakers from around the US wrote letters of concern to the Department of War. Over 50,000 American citizens sent telegrams on behalf of the 101 Club. Members of Congress went directly to the secretary of war urging their release. Labor unions and national civil rights organizations applied additional pressure. Not even the sudden death of President Franklin Delano Roosevelt on April 12 took the pressure off General Hunter and Colonel Selway.

Lawyers arrived from the NAACP prepared to represent the 101 Club as they went in front of a panel of three Army Air Corps officers, one full colonel, and two lieutenant colonels who were sent to investigate the incident. They were assisted by Lieutenant William T. Coleman Jr., a member of the 477th and a Harvard Law student until his education was interrupted by the war.

When it was his turn to face questions, JB chose to stand up and speak for himself. He trusted his own abilities. Of this decision, he said:

> *I wanted to go to med school and I didn't want anything to interfere with me getting help from the [US] Army to go to medical school. So, I just represented myself. I depended on me to get to med school.*

He never remembered the exact words he used to explain that this was not just an issue for Black Americans. He simply told the inquisition what he saw as an obvious truth, that the country could not continue fighting wars with a divided army, not if it intended to continue winning against common enemies. The purpose of having Blacks in the military was to help solve existing problems, not to make more.

After his interview, Coleman complimented JB, calling his words excellent. Coleman should know. After World War II, he returned to Harvard, where he graduated first in his class before becoming the first Black law clerk for the United States Supreme Court. With all those credentials, he still had difficulty being hired. Coleman was finally accepted at Paul, Weiss, Rifkind, Wharton & Garrison, the first major law firm to hire a Black associate. During his career, he worked as part of the NAACP Legal Defense Fund, and in President Gerald R. Ford's cabinet as transportation secretary.

Things got too big for Colonel Selway. Too big for General Hunter, who tried to blame all the problems on the colonel. A few days after the investigators returned to Washington, chief of staff of the US Army, General George Marshall, ordered the release of the 101 officers.

General Hunter insisted on placing a nasty letter of reprimand in the military file of each member of the 101 Club. The letters called each man a disgrace to their country and to their race for having a "stubborn and uncooperative attitude toward authority." Those black marks, placed on their records by a commander more eager to preserve racial segregation than to do his job preparing troops for combat, were supposed to haunt the men for the rest of their lives.

Nothing he couldn't live with, JB decided. At the time, he had no way of knowing the mutiny would become a landmark point for the growing US civil rights movement and lead to the eventual desegregation of the armed forces.

Years later, he told an interviewer for Creighton University's alumni magazine, "I thought what we were doing was proper, and I figured it was the only way to approach the segregation that was throughout the military. It was a big risk, doing what we did. Fortunately, for the good of the country, and for our own good, it turned out well."

Only Second Lieutenant Terry and the two others arrested with him remained in prison. They were charged with mutiny, treason, inciting to riot, conduct unbecoming an officer, disobeying a direct order . . . and jostling a superior officer.

The NAACP sent attorneys to defend the three officers at their court-martial a month later. Theodore Berry, president of the organization's Cincinnati, Ohio, branch and future mayor of Cincinnati, led the defense team. The board assigned to judge the trial consisted of six Black officers. George Levi Knox II, the senior captain at the time, presided over this court-martial. Every white officer called to testify refused to salute those judges. Captain Knox halted the trial again and again so the white officers could be "reminded" that a salute was required.

NAACP branch office in Detroit, Michigan.

The three accused officers denied ever hitting Lieutenant Rogers. Two men had witnesses to their innocence. Terry did not.

In the end, the other two officers were acquitted. Only Second Lieutenant Terry was convicted of "offering violence against a superior officer." He was fined $150, a sizable amount for those days. Other Tuskegee

Airmen took up a collection to pay his fine. They understood what he'd felt and why he'd lost control.

The military also took away the rank of second lieutenant that Terry had worked hard to earn, and kicked him out of the army with a dishonorable discharge. Both acts were meant to leave the man feeling disgraced. Neither was successful. Terry considered them badges of honor.

WAR'S END

JB NEVER MADE IT inside the Freeman Field's officers' club. The entire 477th returned to Godman Field. Their morale was in the toilet. General Hunter had managed to do something none of America's enemies ever accomplished: He put a complete group of airmen out of action.

The Freeman Field Mutiny had one immediate positive result. Colonel Selway and the rest of the all-white leadership of the 477th came to an end. Lieutenant Colonel Benjamin O. Davis Jr. returned from overseas and took over as commander of the

477th. Like a petty bully, General Hunter refused to attend the ceremony where Lieutenant Colonel Davis took command. In order to avoid the possibility of a Black commanding officer presiding over white subordinate officers, every white officer at Godman had been taken from the base a few hours before the ceremony.

As soon as he assumed command, Lieutenant Colonel Benjamin Davis Jr. issued long-overdue promotions that placed several members of the 477th into command and key staff positions. He assured his men that anyone with ambition could go as far as their abilities and performance would take them. Bill Terry described further changes this way:

> *The white folks, they were working in Air Corps*
> *supply. They found out he . . . he's bringing a*
> *whole colored command with him, and they said,*
> *"We refuse to work for him." That's one thing*
> *I can say for him. Davis was not phased [sic] one*

bit by it. He sent for . . . two companies of [Black]
WACS [from Des Moines, Iowa] and brought
them there right away. And, they [the whites]
said, "Well, now we'll go to work for you!" And,
he said, "No. It's too late. We've already got your
replacements."

Morale lifted. Having a leader who believed in their capabilities made every difference. Now all they had to do was concentrate on completing bomber flight training and joining the war effort. General MacArthur was eager for the 477th to join him in the Pacific. The short runways and other difficulties Godman presented for bomber flights still hampered training flights. As a result, training had to be extended for several additional months. Their new date for deployment in the Pacific became the end of August.

Japan surrendered to the Allies on August 14, 1945, only weeks before the 477th was ready to enter the war. World War II officially ended on September 2, 1945.

The Tuskegee Airmen won multiple Distinguished Unit Citations in the skies over Europe and Africa and were credited with over 15,000 combat raids by war's end. Those brave aviators, along with thousands of infantrymen like Jasper Fleming Williams, proved that if you gave a Black man the same training given white men, he could do the same job.

That should not have been a revolutionary idea, but it was to white America in the 1940s. As far as most of America knew, World War II had been a white man's war. Yet over 900,000 Black men donned the olive drab uniform, and countless Black women ended up serving in the military medical corps, or as mechanics and office staff. Even the comics pages in white newspapers omitted the efforts of Black fighters. The only way most civilians found out about the exploits of Black men and women overseas were on the pages of Negro papers like the *Pittsburgh Courier*, the *Journal & Guide*, and the *Chicago Defender*.

Black war correspondents had done their best to publicize the stories of the Red Tails and other Black fighting men. They faced censorship and segregation as part of the job. Their stories might never have won any journalistic prizes, but they made the war easier for Black soldiers and their loved ones.

The military's strict segregation policies actually made Black journalists' jobs a bit simpler. When a Black correspondent arrived at a new sector, he could head directly to locations filled with Black GIs. Several correspondents disobeyed orders to leave their cameras behind, and they became unofficial war photographers. When they started sending combat pictures back to the US, even some white newspapers printed them. John Jordan, a correspondent for the *Journal & Guide*, described what happened to him when he defied regulations and took his camera to the front.

> *Nobody cared much at first. They figured to themselves, "Black papers, who are they competing with anyway?" But when we started sending out combat pictures, with terrific action, all the big papers started using them*

and everyone started wondering where they came from. Even Stars and Stripes *printed my stuff. So they started asking, "Who's this John Jordan?" . . . I received a directive to not carry the camera anymore, and I told them I sure wouldn't. But, I did anyway.*

Correspondents saw to it that stories got out in spite of censorship by an army that did not want to look bad. For example, a military censor in 1945 refused to transmit a story by Black correspondent Deton Brooks about a military swimming pool. The pool was reserved on alternate days for Blacks and for whites. Brooks threatened to have his paper demand an investigation, both of the pool and of the censorship. According to Brooks, the censor's ears turned red, but he filed the story. Even better, shortly after the story was published, the pool was integrated.

Although members of the 477th never had the chance to prove themselves in combat, they won one of the most essential battles of the war. Today, historians of the civil rights movement consider the Freeman Field Mutiny an important step toward full integration of the armed forces. For many of the young men in the 477th, the experience of being part of something larger than themselves so early in life helped push them on to perform even greater deeds in their future lives.

Coleman Young left the military after the war. He returned to Detroit and jumped back into the fight for civil rights. He eventually entered politics and became Detroit's first Black mayor.

Former second lieutenant Roger Terry paid an extremely high price for his participation in the Freeman Field protests. However, he didn't let it stop him from accomplishing great things. Following his dishonorable discharge, he enrolled at Southwestern Law School and earned a law degree. His conviction and dishonorable discharge carried the same weight as a civilian felony conviction, so he could not practice law. He could not even vote. He had to admit to a felony conviction at every job interview. He still became a successful investigator with the Los Angeles

County district attorney's office and worked with the LA probation department.

Terry helped found Tuskegee Airmen Inc. (TAI), an organization designed to draw attention to, and help preserve, the memory of the Tuskegee Airmen for future generations like yours. He served as TAI's president for many years, striving to make the organization a living legacy of the men and women who proved Black people were capable of excelling at tasks segregation claimed they could not. He spent time at Skywalker Ranch in Northern California while serving as a technical advisor for *Red Tails*, the 2012 film produced by George Lucas.

Lieutenant Quentin P. Smith returned to teaching following his discharge. He served as an Indiana guidance counselor and school principal. He earned a master's degree in English and became director of secondary education for the Gary Community School Corporation in Indiana.

Unfortunately, Esteban Hotesse died in a training accident, one of the few accidents the unit ever

Painting of *The Trial of Roger Terry* by Chris Hopkins.

suffered. His B-25 crashed shortly before Japan surrendered. The world forgot about him until the year 2015. A scholar at City University of New York named Edward De Jesus rediscovered the Dominican Tuskegee Airman while working on a research project on Dominican servicemen and women who "made significant contributions to the war effort or who made significant contributions to society." Now his role in fighting for America is known in both New York and the Dominican Republic.

Shortly after V-J Day (Victory in Japan Day, August 14, 1945), the Ku Klux Klan lit a 300-foot cross in Georgia to show they were back in power. Later in August, three Black WACs (Women's Army Corps) were assaulted by the police for taking seats in a white waiting room while waiting for a bus to take them back to their base, Fort Knox, where they worked in the regional hospital. The police beat the women so badly that one, PFC Helen Smith, had to be hospitalized for a week. She was the mother of a Black serviceman stationed overseas.

With the war over, the 99th Pursuit Squadron returned to the States and joined the 477th. The combination was called the 477th Composite Group. Lieutenant Colonel Davis moved the Composite Group to Lockbourne Air Base in Ohio. (Lockbourne was later renamed Rickenbacker Air National Guard Base.) That move met with stiff opposition from men like Don Weaver, editor of the *Columbus Citizen*, who said:

> *This is a fact, that Negroes in this country are considered servants, and we should not send our servants to fight for us because we cannot take the results—such as worshipping them as heroes.*

Local resistance increased after the paper published a story calling the unit a troublemaking group that had already provoked "one riot at Freeman Field . . . when officers of the group attempted to take over the officers club."

They were alone at Lockbourne; the white units that had once filled Lockbourne left to avoid a Black officer as base commander. At first, area residents continued to call the Black pilots troublemakers and lobbied for their removal. Then Colonel Davis started holding weekend air shows. A few years later, when Davis served in the Pentagon, he gained approval to

Thunderbird demonstration team.

create the Air Force Thunderbird aerial demonstration team. If you get a chance to see them fly, you will understand why many of the people of Columbus soon forgot the pilots and crews were Black and only wanted to see more of them in action.

The Tuskegee Airmen enjoyed their independence and worked hard to prove they deserved it. George Levi Knox III, the son of the judge at Terry's court-martial, was only a boy during this time, but he remembered how Lockbourne base always received high ratings during administrative inspections. (An inspection report in 1948 said that Lockbourne, under Davis's leadership, "could well serve as a model for bases in the Air Force.") Young George learned to swim at the base swimming pool. He also enjoyed watching the troops during parades and reviews, even though it was against the rules.

I used to love to watch the troops being reviewed by Colonel Davis . . . we would sneak over and hide under the reviewing stand, you know he's standing up there, we're lying down on the grass looking out between the boards at the parades

and reviews. I loved, loved that.

The men explained, "Everywhere on the base there was evidence of striving for perfection. [Lockbourne was] 'our' base, run, from top to bottom and all in between, by 'us.'"

JB used his time at Lockbourne wisely. While he waited for his own honorable discharge, he attended night classes in physics at nearby Ohio State University. He still needed physics for his premed degree. Then, in 1946, with his discharge papers in hand, he boarded a train for home.

For some Black soldiers, the return home from World War II seemed like a repeat of the return from the First World War. "Tuskegee Airmen often came home to stares of disbelief when they told what they did in the war," said Michael Joseph, a historian with TAI. Many returning Black soldiers learned to keep their experiences to themselves. "It actually got to the point where most of us just did not talk about the experience at all, because no one really believed," one soldier said.

The ships bringing soldiers home from overseas were integrated. Then, when they pulled into port, men were met with signs sending white troops in one direction, Blacks in another. White military men and women found adoring crowds and parades waiting for them. Black soldiers often faced a different welcome, one laced with another wave of anti-Black violence directed at them.

The sight of a Black man in uniform often produced the same effect as waving a red flag in front of a herd of bulls. Hoping to avoid a repeat of the Red Summer, some Southern Black families sent messages to enlisted friends and relatives warning them not to wear their uniforms when they returned home. Not every soldier got the message. Folk artist Woody Guthrie recorded "The Blinding of Isaac Woodard," a song named after a twenty-seven-year-old Black World War II veteran. In February 1946, a police chief in

South Carolina, Lynwood Shull, pulled Isaac from a bus while he was still in uniform, only hours after he had received his honorable discharge. His crime, telling the bus driver, "I'm a man, just like you," after the driver cursed at him and called him boy.

According to a 1946 news article, "Shull was waiting for him at the bus door, he said, and struck him before he could say anything. . . . Two war veterans—a Negro and a white—who were discharged at Augusta the same day as Woodard and rode on the bus with him, testified that the Negro was not drunk and had not created a disturbance."

Chief Shull and his men beat Woodard so badly they gouged one eye completely from its socket. His other eye was left permanently blinded. Thirty-year-old Orson Welles was a major influencer in his day. He frightened half the country with his 1938 radio dramatization of a Martian invasion, *War of the Worlds*. *Citizen Kane*, a movie he wrote, directed, and starred in, has been praised as one of the greatest movies ever made. When he learned what happened to Woodard,

Welles used his influence to deliver a series of radio broadcasts on the soldier's behalf.

I was born a white man, and until a colored man is a full citizen, like me, I haven't the leisure to enjoy the freedom that a colored man risked his life to maintain for me. Until somebody beats me and blinds me, I am in his debt.

Thanks in large part to the efforts of Welles, Chief Shull was identified and arrested. Shull was soon acquitted after a short trial and even shorter jury deliberation (fifteen minutes). All the defense attorney had to do was warn the all-white jury members that convicting the policeman of destroying a Black man's sight meant that white women and children would no longer be safe.

The white judge hearing the case, J. Waties Waring, was appalled by the miscarriage of justice. Although there was nothing he could do about the jury verdict, he chose to devote the rest of his career to fighting

Isaac Woodard, who was beaten and blinded by police, applied for maximum disability benefits. He is shown seated with David Edwards; standing (l to r) Oliver W. Harrington, Edward Nottage, and his mother, Mrs. Isaac Woodard.

against the kind of white supremacy that could leave a crime like this brutal beating unpunished. He attacked Jim Crow laws, even though his stand made his family the targets of threats and violence. Eventually, Judge Waring became involved in a 1951 case involving the rights of Black South Carolina schoolchildren. Although his fellow judges on the case upheld separate but equal, he wrote a fiery dissenting opinion based on the Fourteenth Amendment. Years later, that opinion became the basis of the argument used by Thurgood Marshall before the Supreme Court in *Brown v. Board of Education*, which toppled separate but equal.

Anti-Black violence grew so brutal, civil rights activists got together to form the National Emergency Committee Against Mob Violence. It was the Black Lives Matter organization of its time, and membership included former First Lady Eleanor Roosevelt. The committee petitioned President Truman for a federal anti-lynching law. That ended up being yet another failed attempt. There have been over 240 attempts to pass one since 1901. As of 2021, the United States still has no federal anti-lynching law. The latest attempt, the Emmett Till Antilynching Act, passed in the House of Representatives in 2020, but ended up stalled in the Senate.

When JB spoke of his war experiences, fellow Black Americans listened to him. Many of his mother's young students looked up at him with faces filled with a sense of pride and possibility as they asked if he could really fly an airplane. He enjoyed making lights shine in their eyes as he told them of his experiences.

He arrived home to find his father gravely ill. Jasper Williams had become increasingly upset once his eldest son was shipped overseas for a country that refused to pass an anti-lynching law. He grew so enraged that he suffered a stroke and never fully recovered. At least he lived long enough to see his sons return. "It is my joy that my husband lived to see one son become a doctor, and the other two well on their way," Clara Belle said. He died in 1946 at the age of seventy-three.

Being home returned JB to the perils of being a middle son, squashed between brothers with plenty to boast about. Elder brother Jasper had graduated college with a degree in business administration before the war began. By war's end, he had been promoted from second to full lieutenant. He also held a place in the OCS Hall of Fame. Plus, Jasper was the only family member who had experienced actual combat duty, earning two battle stars in the process. He never spoke much about his experiences to his family, and never even told what he did to get in the Hall of Fame.

Younger brother Charles Lee had leapfrogged over JB, becoming NMSU's second Black graduate ever by completing a bachelor's degree during the war. He then attended Howard University College of Medicine in Washington, DC. His advisor suggested he volunteer for the army medical corps. As a volunteer, the army paid for him to complete medical school. Charles returned from his service as the first Williams brother to hold an MD degree.

THE WAR FOR HEALTH CARE

THE END OF WORLD War II thrust JB into a new struggle. In some ways, he spent his life going from one battlefield to another. Freeman Field. Medical school. Medical practice. Life was all about struggle.

The American health care system made little room for Black medical professionals. Black students found medical schools highly competitive because there were so few spots available to them. An earlier purge of medical schools had closed almost every Black medical school in the United States.

The purge started in 1910, when the American Medical Association (AMA) hired a man named Abraham Flexner to examine undergraduate medical education. Mr. Flexner visited all 155 medical schools in the United States. The report he issued concluded there were too many of them. Especially too many Black medical schools. His report claimed Blacks needed "schools where hygiene rather than surgery, for example, is strongly accentuated." Extremely bad news for a future surgeon like James. Only two Black medical schools survived the purge: Howard University College of Medicine in DC and Meharry Medical College in Nashville. Black student nurses faced the same difficulties when they tried to find training.

Flexner's report also claimed Black doctors were only qualified to serve as assistants to white doctors. That left few white medical schools willing to accept Black students. The number of trained Black doctors plummeted, just in time for the 1918 flu pandemic to overwhelm the scarce medical resources available to the Black community. Some whites even tried to blame the illness and death on the Great Migration. A March 5, 1917, headline from a Chicago newspaper blared, "Rush of Negroes to City Starts Health Inquiry."

The pandemic's third wave hit the year JB was born. He was too young to remember, but evidence of the devastation lay in the hundreds of graves with the same year of death that filled El Paso cemeteries. He likely heard about it in songs schoolgirls chanted as they jumped rope:

> *I had a little bird*
> *And its name was Enza*
> *I opened the window*
> *And in-flew-Enza*

Shortly after World War II ended, Congress passed the Hospital Survey and Construction Act, also known as the Hill-Burton Act (named after the two congressmen who sponsored it). The new law was supposed to improve the medical situation. Hill-Burton provided federal money for parts of the US that had a shortage of hospital beds. That money could be used to construct new hospitals, nursing homes, and other health care facilities, or to modernize and improve existing facilities.

Although Hill-Burton helped a lot of poor people, it contained a racist underbelly. The law codified separate but equal in health care. Black community members could be excluded. In some parts of America, Jim Crow laws said that no matter how sick or badly injured Black patients were, the races could not intermingle.

Few white medical professionals were willing to disobey Jim Crow, not even when obeying meant violating their Hippocratic oath. White-only hospitals refused to admit Blacks, even if the nearest "Colored" hospital was miles away. White nurses who wanted to help a Black patient could lawfully be ordered to stop. Biracial facilities, called deluxe Jim Crow by the NAACP, did admit Black patients, but placed them in segregated wards located in undesirable locations such as unheated attics and damp basements.

How was *anyone* supposed to get well under those conditions?

This was the reality James Buchanan faced when he resumed his premed studies at NMSU. He kept his nose in books, always studying, and soon earned his bachelor of science degree in biochemistry. Then it was time to find a position in a medical school. JB explained, "I went for an interview [at Meharry Medical College] and [the president] looked up at me and said, 'You probably should go into another field,' and that was the interview that he gave me. And I did everything I could to keep from kicking him over . . ." He laughed before adding, "Then I wrote to Howard to get in med school and they turned me down . . ."

At that point, things might have appeared hopeless to someone less determined. JB kept applying, even to schools that had never accepted a Black medical student before. He persuaded the Creighton University School of Medicine in Nebraska to accept him as its first Black medical student.

He spent day after day without seeing anyone who looked like him. Life at Creighton might not have always been smooth, but at least his fellow students didn't act like the cadets at West Point did with Benjamin Davis Jr. and try to ostracize him as a way to drive him out.

He felt pressure to answer every question correctly. White students could have their mistakes lost in the crowd of sameness. He stood out just by entering a room. He could have been one of the specimens students studied under their microscopes. If he messed up, that would be what others remembered about him. Failure on his part could result in future Black students being refused acceptance at the school. That meant he could not, would not fail.

Fortunately, he remained self-assured. He knew he could do anything the others could do—including amusing the nuns at the Jesuit university.

One night, he received an emergency call summoning him to the hospital. He jumped from bed and dressed in the dark before rushing from his room. He put on a hat but did not remember to remove the knitted sleeping cap he used to keep his head warm while he slept. A nun entered while he was on the elevator, and he removed his hat to be polite. That's when he realized he still had the sleeping cap on his head. She averted her eyes, leaving him wondering if she was horrified by the sight of him, or entertained by his embarrassment.

Sometimes he had to listen to racist pseudoscience masquerading as truth. That included the belief that Black people did not feel pain the way white people did. Someone might point toward so-called experts like James Marion Sims, a nineteenth-century doctor. His work earned him the title of "father of gynecology." But achieving that meant Sims abandoned his medical oath, *primum non nocere*, or, "first, do no harm." Beginning in 1845, he performed experimental surgery on female slaves. His first victim was seventeen-year-old Anarcha. By 1849, he had performed thirty unanesthetized

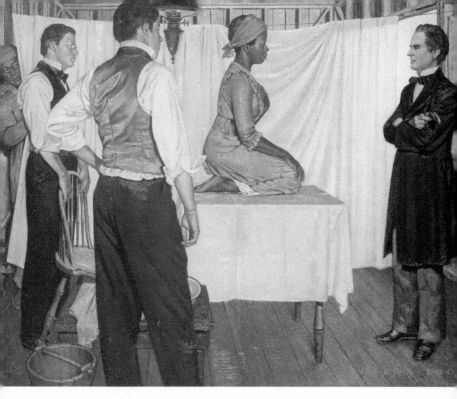

Illustration of Dr. J. Marion Sims with Anarcha by Robert Thom.

surgeries on the girl in his attempts to perfect his technique. Anesthesia was costly and reserved for his white patients. He even claimed Anarcha and his other Black victims were eager to participate in his experiments, as if any enslaved woman was ever given a choice about submitting her body to his knives.

For a long time, the enslaved girls and women Sims experimented on were largely forgotten. Then, in September 2021, a monument was erected to them in Montgomery, Alabama. The monument includes figures of Anarcha, Lucy, and Betsey, three of the many slaves Sims used. They were the only slaves he bothered to name when he wrote his notes.

Popular opinion, and some medical professionals, claimed that Blacks were biologically, physiologically, and morally inferior, in spite of obvious evidence that opinion was wrong. Beneath a thin layer of pigment and a few superficial external features, all races were the same. A heart from a Black chest was anatomically identical to one from a white person. Nevertheless, there were doctors like Dr. J. Madison Taylor, from Temple University's medical school, who voiced his erroneous opinion in 1915, telling other doctors that Blacks were structurally maladapted to live in Northern cities. Opinions like these spread faster and farther than facts.

At least JB could relax and leave that behind when he went off campus and spent time among Omaha's Black residents. He could talk and laugh without needing to watch his words. People shared their thoughts with him, too. He listened to many complaints about the university, especially about the dental school.

Dental school students worked on the teeth of the people in town. This gave them practical experience, and provided low-cost dental care to local residents. But dental students would only fill cavities for white patients. With Black patients, students would just pull teeth, which demonstrated the absurdity of segregation.

JB went to the school's dental clinic pretending to need a tooth filled. The lady in charge repeated what the townspeople had told him: "We'll pull it but we won't fill it." When he asked how long this had been the practice, she replied, "Since I've been here, fifteen years."

"Don't you think that's wrong?" he asked. "I'm a Catholic and I'm at this school, they have a cross on the top of this building." (Shortly after being admitted, JB converted to Catholicism.)

Her rude and abrasive reply was that students didn't want to be bothered treating Blacks. She told him, "You people don't belong here."

After his army experiences, he knew the power of peaceful protest. He used that knowledge while confronting the president of the dental school to complain about the segregated practice. The dental school's president made the woman apologize. Shortly afterward, the Creighton University School of Dentistry admitted its first Black dental student.

Back in Las Cruces, Jasper's well-drilling business was thriving. Then one day an engine exploded and broke six of his ribs. While Jasper recuperated, JB and Charles talked him into going back to NMSU for premed studies and becoming a doctor with them. Apparently he, too, had always had an interest in medicine. JB helped him get admitted to Creighton University School of Medicine. Now he was no longer alone at school.

And then JB found real companionship. His ever-expanding quest for more knowledge led him to take a class as an extern at the nearby University of Nebraska Medical Center. Externing gave him practical clinical experience and exposed him to a new set of experienced medical professionals. It also exposed him to Willeen Brown, a student at the University of Nebraska.

Willeen was described as "a very elegant lady, very beautiful and classy and very outgoing." She and her two sisters sang and were "really pretty in different ways and so they made quite a splash" in Omaha.

Willeen had her own experience of life as one of the few Black children in a mostly white city. Years earlier, her school class planned a visit to a swimming pool, only to find that officials at the pool would not let them enter if the Black child was included.

She grew into an outgoing and politically active undergraduate who attracted JB's attention. He began searching for excuses to see her. When he discovered she didn't know how to drive, he volunteered to be her teacher. Willeen Brown made the quiet, science-minded James Buchanan Williams feel at ease. She loved talking about a variety of subjects. Both were politically aware and might even have been called radical. She talked, he listened. They fell in love.

As his graduation day approached, JB was accepted for an internship at Provident Hospital and Training School in Chicago. Built in 1891 by Dr. Dale Williams (no relation), Provident Hospital was the first African American owned and operated hospital in the US. Dr. Williams started Provident to help Black women who wanted to become nurses and could not find a place that would train them. Provident was one of the few places in the country where Black interns, residents, and nurses could train and find work. JB's brother Charles did both his internship and residency at Provident Hospital before accepting a full-time staff position.

Many of the doctors at Provident had been trained in hospitals outside the country. Interning with them would give valuable insight into techniques used across the globe. That left JB happy to be heading north to work with them. The problem was Willeen. She was only nineteen, and he was asking her to marry him and accompany him across the country.

Time froze as he waited for her answer. She was much younger than he. His mother had been much younger than his father, and she said yes. That meant he had a chance.

A moment later, she spoke the word that made his heart begin beating again. They married in 1951, the day before he graduated with his MD degree.

After he completed a year as a Chicago intern, Dr. James Williams and Willeen returned to Nebraska. There he entered Creighton's surgical residency program. Once again he broke a color barrier, becoming the first Black surgical resident at any non-Black school in America. And then he went further, becoming the first Creighton graduate to pass the American Board of Surgery exam on the first attempt.

When he finished his residency and a master's degree in surgery, James Williams took his wife and new daughter, Brenda Joyce, born in 1953, off to Canada. He received a grant that sent him to the Royal Victoria Hospital at McGill University, in Montreal, for additional training. Every time he studied with a new group of experts, he learned more and found opportunities to practice new techniques.

Doctors of the Williams family, November 1980. From left to right: Jasper Williams Jr., Jasper Williams Sr., James Buchanan Williams, Charles Williams Jr., and Charles Williams Sr.

McGill's excellent teaching and research programs are recognized all over the world. He sought out every opportunity to add to his medical arsenal. Being the best meant having to give at least 110 percent more than the average white doctor just to have the same chance at success.

From McGill he returned to Chicago after accepting a job as St. Bernard Hospital's first Black physician. He was becoming a specialist in breaking new ground. Poor Willeen must have felt like she was on a yo-yo while she packed to return to the Windy City with their three-year-old daughter, Brenda.

The Williams family eventually settled into a town house in Hyde Park, an integrated neighborhood located on Chicago's South Side. In addition to being integrated, Hyde Park remains one of the most culturally diverse areas in the city. The neighborhood houses the University of Chicago and is encircled by landmarks like the DuSable Museum of African American History, the Oriental Institute of the University of Chicago, and Chicago's Museum of

Science and Industry. The Williams family now included two children, Brenda Joyce Williams and son James Buchanan Williams II. Hyde Park provided the atmosphere and intellectual stimulation they wanted for their children.

Dr. Jasper Williams also traveled to Chicago for an internship at Provident Hospital. He remained there for his residency. After doing some postgraduate study at the University of Wisconsin and at Harvard University, he joined brother Charles Williams on the staff at Provident as an obstetrician-gynecologist.

Meanwhile, their mother, Clara Belle Williams, continued taking graduate-level classes at NMSU until well into the 1950s. When she retired from teaching at the age of sixty-five, the independent woman moved into a Chicago apartment to be near her sons and grandchildren. She quickly settled in as matriarch, with her living room as the center of family life for Jasper, James, Charles, and their growing families.

THE NATIONAL MEDICAL
ASSOCIATION

PIONEERS ARE USUALLY THE first individuals in any field of inquiry or enterprise. They initiate, instigate, set things in motion, take the plunge. Being a pioneer can be exhilarating. It always requires a great deal of work and the ability to confront adversity. Most of all, it can be very lonely.

When Dr. James Williams first joined St. Bernard Hospital, a number of white doctors shunned him. One day when he walked into the dressing room where a group of doctors were gathered, a white urologist loudly remarked, "Things are getting awfully dark around here. I'm going to have to find me some other hospital to go to."

Dr. Williams did not react, outwardly. He continued doing his job, swallowed his feelings, and ignored the racism of other doctors who might not want him around. He concentrated on building up his surgical skills and his reputation for excellence.

A few years later, the same urologist who once insulted JB had an accident while working on a patient. He could not stop the bleeding, and his patient lay dying on the operating table. The situation grew so dire, a priest was called to the operating room to give the patient last rites. When Dr. Williams learned of the situation, he quickly scrubbed in and took over. He stopped the bleeding and saved the patient's life.

In a fairy tale, the urologist would have learned to respect his Black coworker after this. He and Dr. Williams would shake hands and become forever friends. In reality, the urologist walked out of the operating room without saying a word.

His situation was not unique. Many Black patients faced a similar bias from white doctors. Some were given only cursory examinations by those doctors or told their real problem lay with their lifestyle choices and left untreated. Often doctors assumed Black patients exaggerated their symptoms and level of pain. Many of those physicians remembered hearing that Black people did not experience pain the same way white people did while in medical school. These patients learned to seek out Dr. Williams as someone who would listen, believe, and help.

The separate but equal policy dominated professional organizations like the American Medical Association. The AMA spent decades ignoring Black doctors and the health issues of Black people. Even before World War II, a doctor at New York's Harlem Hospital noted, "The AMA has demonstrated as much interest in the health of the Negro as Hitler has in the health of the Jew."

Some AMA chapters included the word *white* in their admissions requirements, documenting their decision that no Black doctors need apply. Since membership in a state chapter was a requirement for membership in the AMA, this shut out many Black physicians, like Dr. Nixon back in El Paso.

In response to the practices of the AMA that excluded medical professionals of African descent, a group banded together in 1895 to form the National Medical Association, NMA. The NMA is an organization dedicated to providing its members with mutual cooperation and assistance. There are no ethnic or gender requirements for membership. Inclusion is the goal, and they welcome anyone legally and honorably engaged in the practice of medicine. Today, the organization represents more than 30,000 Black physicians and targets health issues specific to minority groups and the medically underserved.

The Williams brothers joined the Cook County Physicians Association (CCPA), the Chicagoland chapter of the National Medical Association. When the NMA advised members to start their own hospitals and clinics, the Williams brothers embraced the idea. They pooled their resources and founded the Williams Clinic, which served an area on Chicago's far South Side holding a large number of low-income Black and Hispanic residents.

When their old family friend, Dr. Nixon, learned about the new clinic, he told the brothers, "You ought to build it here, in El Paso." He was only partly joking.

As battles raged inside the halls of medicine, the world outside began to change. Sixty years after the *Plessy v. Ferguson* ruling affirming segregation, the Supreme Court agreed to look at a new separate but equal case, *Brown v. Board of Education of Topeka.*

A man named Oliver Brown filed a lawsuit against the Topeka, Kansas, board of education on behalf of his daughter, Linda Brown. The all-white elementary school near her home refused to let her attend. The lawsuit said the schools for Black children were not equal. Thurgood Marshall, head of the NAACP Legal Defense and Educational Defense, argued the case in front of the Supreme Court. Utilizing an opinion voiced by

Judge J. Waties Waring in a similar case, the lawyers argued that letting public schools refuse to educate Black children violated the equal protection of the laws guaranteed by the Fourteenth Amendment.

The Supreme Court judges ruled in favor of Linda Brown on May 7, 1954, reversing *Plessy*. The ruling stated that "the doctrine of 'separate but equal' has no place in public education." That established a legal

Mrs. Nettie Hunt and her daughter, Nikie, sitting on the steps of the Supreme Court, holding a newspaper declaring the 1954 decision banning school segregation.

precedent that civil rights activists were ready to use to overturn segregation laws in education, housing, and health care. If segregation was bad for children, it was bad for everyone.

The National Medical Association put this decision to work right away. Members coordinated sit-ins, marches, and picket lines across the country. The editor of the *Journal of the National Medical Association* wrote,

> *With the deadline for social justice long overdue,*
> *Negroes in the medical and allied*
> *professions threw themselves into the battle to*
> *close the citizenship gap in the health field.*

The organization began immediate discussions on ways to integrate health care for patients and providers. Over a seven-year period, beginning in 1957, they sponsored annual meetings called the Imhotep National Conferences on Hospital Integration. They selected the name Imhotep for two reasons:

First, as a reminder that a dark skin was

associated with distinction in medicine

before that of any other color. This will serve

to emphasize the dignity of the approach to

the problem of the sponsoring organizations.

Secondly, because Imhotep means, "He who

cometh in peace." In a time of emotional tension,

the sponsoring organizations wanted everyone to

know that they "come in peace."

The yearly conferences were held until 1963 and pro-vided opportunities for medical professionals to share strategies for ending segregation in health care. The Williams brothers were vocal participants. The American Medical Association was invited to be part of the Imhotep initiative. They initially agreed to join, but then were absent from many of the meetings. Worse still, as the years progressed, the NMA and AMA often found themselves on opposing sides in the fight against discrimination.

The year 1963 proved to be one of transition in America. On television, *The Beverly Hillbillies*, a show about a newly rich family shaking up the neighborhood, was number one. Cell phones did not exist. Neither did Apple, Microsoft, Google, Instagram, or TikTok. "Dominique," a French-language song performed by a Belgian singer known as the Singing Nun, became a hit.

The year was also a turning point in the struggle for civil rights. January set the tone when George Wallace, then governor of Alabama, ranted for all the world to see and hear, "Segregation today . . . segregation tomorrow, segregation forever."

As winter turned to spring, scenes of battles between authorities and protesters filled the news. In Birmingham, Alabama, segregationist Theophilus Eugene "Bull" Connor gave orders for the police and fire departments to turn high-pressure fire hoses and dogs against peaceful protesters. The dogs had no choice and obeyed their handlers. The police and firemen had a choice and still decided to obey orders to punish people for seeking their rights. Water from their hoses knocked people to the ground like hurricane winds. Their victims included children, some as young as six. Some kids joined hands in a human chain in an attempt to keep their balance and stay together, but the rocket-like blasts of water dragged them apart and sent their small bodies whirling down the streets.

The violence went viral. Images of children scream-ing in pain were broadcast across the globe night after night. People watched as Black Americans were attacked for the same crime that had led to the arrest of the Black officers at Freeman Field—defying segregation orders.

James and Willeen Williams were among the many Black Americans who observed the events in Alabama and other parts of the country, including their home, Chicago. Black children in Chicago staged a school strike, trying to change a system that bypassed the spirit of the *Brown v. Board of Education* ruling.

Brenda Joyce observed the turmoil through adoles-cent eyes. Even though she attended the University of Chicago Laboratory School, a private school that pro-vided its students with everything, including small class sizes, Brenda knew things were different for her friends who attended Chicago public schools. The stories they told her sounded a lot like the tales of the segregated school her father had had to attend back in the church basement.

Her friends spoke of overcrowded schools forced to hold classes in the cafeteria or gym, and sometimes out in hallways. Sometimes students were forced to attend school in shifts, one group in the morning, the other in the afternoon. Or try to learn inside one of the dreaded Willis Wagons, aluminum trailers used as mobile classrooms that grew stuffy and hot when the sun shone down on the metal sides. They were called Willis Wagons after then-Chicago superintendent of schools Benjamin Willis. He parked those trailers in the playgrounds and parking lots of overcrowded Black schools to avoid having to transfer Black students into uncrowded white schools. De facto segregation.

Willeen Williams took Brenda and her little brother to see some of the local protests. Dr. James Williams tried to explain, but the surgeon who saved lives and trained other doctors had trouble finding words. Nothing, not even years of education, provides Black parents with a good explanation for how human beings could mistreat others because of skin color.

In the second half of 1963, then-president of the National Medical Association Dr. W. Montague Cobb lost patience at the lack of change, and with the AMA. With or without AMA participation, the time had come for political action.

> *For seven years we have invited them [the AMA] to sit down with us and solve the problem. The high professional and economic levels of these bodies and the altruistic religious principles according to which they are supposed to operate seem to have meant nothing. By their refusal to confer they force action by crisis. And now events have passed beyond them. The initiative offered is no longer theirs to accept.*

The NMA chose to use federal funding as leverage and went after an amendment to remove the Hill-Burton Act's separate but equal loophole. Black Americans paid their taxes like everyone else. The amendment would withhold federal funds from any medical facility where racial segregation or discrimination of any form was allowed. Hospitals would be required to treat patients and staff equally or lose millions.

Dr. James Williams was one of the Black doctors selected to head for Washington on August 1, 1963, to lobby the president of the United States, John F. Kennedy, for legislative action. He was forced to obtain a special clearance to enter the White House because of Freeman Field and the reprimand that remained on his service record.

The president approached him. "He came over and kidded me and said, 'If you don't fight for your rights, you won't get any.'" Dr. Williams wasn't surprised to hear those words. He was sure Kennedy had received a briefing about his part in the mutiny.

Any jitters the doctors felt vanished as they explained their position to the president. They reminded Kennedy that barely a month earlier, events shaking the country had led him to admit that America faced a moral crisis. After the "segregation forever" governor of Alabama physically blocked three Black students from entering the all-white University of Alabama, the president had to send in the National Guard to protect the students' right to attend school. Kennedy gave a speech, saying:

> We are confronted primarily with a moral issue. It is as old as the scriptures and is as clear as the American Constitution. The heart of the question is whether all Americans are to be afforded equal rights and equal opportunities, whether we are going to treat our fellow Americans as we want to be treated.

The NMA's lobbying effort helped talk President Kennedy into backing the amendment. Although he

Thirty physicians and laymen attending the NAACP convention were assigned to march in front of the Chicago headquarters of the American Medical Association (AMA), in protest of "ineffective approach to the problems of segregation and inequality in the field of health."

was assassinated only a few months later, his successor, President Lyndon B. Johnson, continued to support the changes. Title VI of the Civil Rights Act of 1964 halted the distribution of federal funds to any medical facility that practiced any form of segregation.

Title VI succeeded by convincing institutions and agencies they would benefit more from voluntarily complying than by sticking with Jim Crow and losing federal money. The goal had never been to withhold funds for noncompliance, it was to make hospitals *want* to comply. Adults sometimes say federal money comes with strings attached. That is not always a bad thing. In this case, the strings were the requirement that everyone be treated the same. For the most part, it worked. Things did not change overnight, but medical facilities that needed federal money (which was most of them) desegregated.

With discrimination in government-funded health programs outlawed, there was no need for further Imhotep conferences. But one success did not mean the work of the NMA was done. The organization continued to engage in civil rights activities intended to eliminate disparities in health care. Their actions included everything from supporting voter registration campaigns to picketing the segregated AMA.

President John F. Kennedy standing in the Oval Office of the White House with a group of African American physicians and surgeons who are members of the National Medical Association (NMA).

Today, the NMA continues working to improve the health of America's minority populations, and to make cultural competency training a part of medical education for all health care professionals.

The Williams brothers remained NMA members, with Dr. Jasper Williams serving as NMA president in 1975. Some AMA chapters continued to exclude Black doctors from their ranks until well into the twentieth century. The AMA finally admitted its history of racial bias in 1968. Still, it wasn't until 2008 that the AMA issued a formal apology to America's Black doctors for the way it had treated them.

MEDICAL PRACTICE

Dr. James Buchanan Williams became the first Black chief of surgery at St. Bernard Hospital and a professor of surgery at the University of Illinois. He served as chairman of the Illinois Medical Disciplinary Board, investigating complaints against physicians. His patient list included a member of the first group of Black paratroopers, World War II's

555th Parachute Infantry patch.

Dubbed Operation Firefly, the 555th "Triple Nickles" Parachute Infantry Battalion parachuted into forest fires in the Pacific Northwest caused by Japanese balloon bombs.

555th Parachute Infantry Battalion, nicknamed "the Triple Nickles" in honor of the Buffalo Soldiers and the buffalo on the back of a five-cent coin. Based at Camp Pendleton in Oregon, the 555th participated in the top secret Operation Firefly, serving their country as smoke jumpers fighting fires started by incendiary balloons sent over the Pacific from Japan.

Dr. Williams became the first surgeon to save the life of an infant shot in the abdomen and chest while still inside his mother's womb. Thanks to his work removing the bullet and restarting the child's heart, the newborn grew into a lively and curious little boy. The

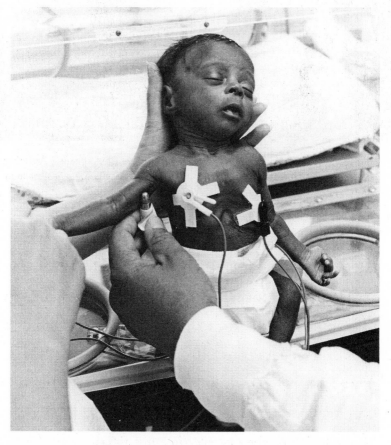

Dr. Williams shows a .38-caliber bullet, the kind that tore through infant Kevin Ruffin's unborn body.

237

Williams family attended his birthday parties for years afterward.

Another of his patients was musician McKinley Morganfield. If you don't know who he is, try streaming a song by Grammy-winning singer/songwriter Muddy Waters. He was often called the father of modern Chicago Blues, music that expresses a universal emotion that can be upbeat, positive, even happy. Relax, close your eyes, and let some of his music flow. You may soon find some of your problems no longer feel quite so heavy.

When civil rights icon the Reverend Dr. Martin Luther King Jr. moved to Chicago in 1966 to expand his civil rights activities in the North, he became Dr. Williams's most famous patient. Although he only saw Dr. King on three occasions, that was enough to grab the attention of J. Edgar Hoover, the director of the Federal Bureau of Investigation (FBI). He saw Martin Luther King as a communist threat and kept the reverend under almost constant surveillance. Those were the days of rotary phones and waiting to

Dr. Martin Luther King Jr., center front, marches for civil rights, arms linked in a line of men, in the March on Washington on August 28, 1963.

hear a dial tone before dialing a number. Sometimes, when Williams family members picked up the phone receiver to make a call, they heard clicking sounds before the dial tone started, a telltale sign their line was being tapped. The fearless Dr. Williams responded by deliberately voicing negative remarks about Hoover for the listening FBI operatives.

Dr. Williams made plenty of time to relax and enjoy life with his family. Fun time included ski trips in the colder months. During summer vacations, they climbed into their motor home and went on fishing trips, sometimes on Lake Michigan, sometimes traveling across the border to Canada's Lake Louise. On other occasions, the family vacationed in Jamaica, a Caribbean island nation of good weather and sandy beaches. Dr. Williams went fishing in Lake Michigan on a boat he named *Estrellita*, which means "Little Star," from the Spanish he learned in his youth.

His younger brother, Dr. Charles Lee Williams, became the chief of medicine at Provident Hospital. He was a colorful character known for talking about his most famous patient, Muhammad Ali, the great heavyweight champion boxer. (Dr. Charles is referenced in Ali's autobiography, *The Greatest*.) He worked nights at the Williams clinic, arriving at six p.m. to serve patients who could not get away from their jobs during the day. Charles relaxed by going scuba diving and taking long rides on his motorcycle.

Older brother Dr. Jasper Fleming Williams became the first Black chair of obstetrics and gynecology at St. Bernard Hospital. He was an avid aviation enthusiast and earned a license allowing him to fly single-engine planes. He went on to serve as an aviation medical examiner and an accident investigator for the Federal Aviation Administration (FAA).

His love of flying also led him to join a group called the Flying Black Medics. The group included doctors, nurses, pharmacists, social workers, dieticians, paramedics, and biochemists from Chicago. Like today's Doctors Without Borders, they brought

Flying Black Medics at Midway Airport.

medical care and health education to Cairo, Illinois, a remote community at the southernmost tip of the state. Cairo's hospital had never applied for state or federal resources. No federal money meant they avoided having to comply with Title VI of the Civil Rights Act, which prohibited discrimination. It also meant illness in the Black community and the poor white community in their area often went untreated.

The Flying Black Medics set up a field hospital in the basement of Cairo's Ward Chapel AME Church. Inside, they examined hundreds of people. Some needed immediate treatment for serious yet undiagnosed problems like congenital (present from birth) heart conditions. Dr. Jasper Williams had charge of the women's disease unit in the basement hospital and gave an educational talk on health care to community members.

Clara Belle Williams accumulated her own share of accolades and awards. In addition to being awarded the title of "grandma" by clinic patients, she was named the outstanding mother and businesswoman of the year in 1966. She received a National Medical

Association Scroll of Merit in 1977. That same year, The National Education Association inducted her into the Teachers Hall of Fame.

A few years later, the Williams family watched her receive a diploma. New Mexico State University officials, recognizing the injustice the school did to its first Black graduate, presented Clara Belle Williams with an honorary doctorate for her overall service to mankind in 1980. No one boycotted this graduation. Well-wishers filled NMSU's auditorium for the ceremony and her speech, part of which was made in the Spanish she had learned as a child. The university apologized for the treatment she received during her years as a student there.

MUTINY'S FINAL ACTS

THE EFFECTS OF RACISM can be as blatant as denying a person the right to sit and enjoy a comfortable evening with their friends for no other reason than the color of their skin. It can also be subtle, like the fact that the army let almost fifty years pass before removing the letters of reprimand from the files of the officers involved in the Freeman Field Mutiny.

That happened in 1995, when the air force reversed the actions taken against the Freeman Field mutineers. Rodney Coleman, former Assistant Secretary of the Air Force for Manpower, Reserve Affairs, Installations, and

Environment, made an announcement at a meeting of Tuskegee Airmen Inc. He said this about the members of the 101 Club and the three officers accused of jostling:

> *The 104 officers involved in the so-called*
> *"mutiny" have lived the last 50 years knowing*
> *they were right in what they did—yet feeling*
> *the stigma of an unfair stain on their records*
> *because they were American fighting men,*
> *too—and wanted to be treated as such.*

"My father didn't have much to say about that," JB's daughter said after the announcement. "It was like, OK, that's done."

Roger Terry, the only man convicted during the mutiny, received a full pardon, and had his rank of second lieutenant restored and his fine refunded. For the first time in fifty years, one month, and two days, he could legally vote. You might think he might still be bitter. Instead, Terry declared that act removed a weight he had been carrying ever since the ordeal. He added, "All my hatred went away. All of it."

Sometimes an apology can mean everything.

Sadly, neither Dr. Jasper Williams nor Clara Belle Williams were present to see the day. Ten years earlier, Dr. Jasper Williams was piloting his private plane, returning home from a vacation with one of his sons and a family friend. The plane crashed in a cornfield near Bloomington, Indiana, killing everyone aboard.

Clara Belle Williams passed away in 1994, three months before her 109th birthday. For over a century, her life stood as a shining example of overcoming adversity. That long-ago little girl who worked hard enough to receive a scholarship left a mighty legacy. She educated hundreds of children and adults in Las Cruces while simultaneously raising three doctors who saved the lives of countless patients. She produced numerous grandchildren, many of whom became doctors, journalists, and educators working to improve the world. Clara Belle believed knowledge was like oxygen, something smart people never got enough of. She passed that belief to her children, grandchildren, and almost everyone she met throughout her life.

Excellent work for a sharecropper's daughter.

Charles and James sold the Williams Clinic shortly after their mother died. James retired in 2004 after practicing surgery for forty-six years. He returned to Las Cruces, New Mexico, with Willeen, happy to once again breathe the air of his childhood.

Dr. James Williams was three years into his retirement when he received an unexpected notice. The United States Congress voted unanimously to award the Congressional Gold Medal to the men and women who served as Tuskegee Airmen. Yes, there were female Tuskegee Airmen, members of the ground crews and office staff of the 99th and 332nd. President George W. Bush invited the surviving Tuskegee Airmen to the capital so the nation could officially recognize their accomplishments in fighting fascism abroad and racism at home.

The Williams family boarded a plane and headed to DC. There Dr. Williams joined a group of almost 400 elderly Tuskegee Airmen in the US Capitol Building. Some were in wheelchairs or used walkers. The air felt alive with energy. Pride kept men's backs straight.

People attending the medal ceremony included House Speaker Nancy Pelosi, United States represen-tatives and senators, and the late General Colin L. Powell, former chairman of the Joint Chiefs of Staff and former secretary of state—the first Black American to hold either post. In an emotion-filled voice, Powell thanked the surviving Tuskegee Airmen for what they accomplished for all Black Americans, including him-self, saying, "I benefited from what you and so many others did . . . I know in the depth of my heart that the only reason I'm able to stand proudly before you today is because you stood proudly for America sixty years ago."

President Bush spoke about the Double V Campaign during the medal presentation. He reminded everyone that the men returned from defending their country to face unreturned salutes and other indignities at home. Then the president of the United States saluted the

Tuskegee Airmen, saying, "I would like to offer a gesture to help atone for all the unreturned salutes and unforgivable indignities. And so, on behalf of the Office I hold and a country that honors you, I salute you for the service to the United States of America."

Dr. Williams could not stop beaming during the ceremony. He fingered his medal and said in a soft voice, "I think all that was pretty amazing."

After the ceremony, he toured the Smithsonian National Air and Space Museum with his wife and children. Everywhere they went, white and Black people noticed his Tuskegee Airman cap. They stepped close to shake his hand and thank him for his service. On the plane trip back to Las Cruces, the airline bumped James and Willeen Williams up to first class.

Two years later, Dr. James Williams received another invitation that sent him back to Washington, DC. Although he was ninety years old, he couldn't ignore the opportunity to see another result of the changes he helped initiate. He and over 100 other surviving

Tuskegee Airmen endured January air so cold it turned their breaths frosty. The Tuskegee Airmen had reserved seats near the front. They were present to bear witness to one of the most significant moments in American history, the inauguration of the nation's first African American president.

Dr. Williams looked around at the other DOTA, Documented Original Tuskegee Airmen, surrounding him. Many old friends were missing. The list of Lonely Eagles, Tuskegee Airmen who had passed away, grew longer almost every day. "I never thought I would see this," he told his daughter, Brenda, who attended with him. "I'm glad the country has grown to the point it could accept this."

"That was really special," she said later. "All of those Tuskegee Airmen were so stoic. It was freezing that day. All of them were in their 90s and nobody complained."

Barack Obama, the forty-fourth president of the United States, put his hand on Lincoln's Bible and took the oath of office. Dr. Williams, the descendent of enslaved men and women, people who fought to survive and somehow managed to thrive during the Jim Crow years, stared intently. He held his breath as President Obama reminded people that he was the son of a man who would never have been served in local restaurants sixty years earlier.

This is the meaning of our liberty and our creed, why men and women and children of every race and every faith can join in celebration across this magnificent mall; and why a man whose father less than 60 years ago might not have been served in a local restaurant can now stand before you to take a most sacred oath.

After the ceremony ended, Dr. James Williams turned to his daughter and smiled. He uttered his usual understatement: "Obama gave a good speech."

LEGACY

JAMES BUCHANAN WILLIAMS JOINED the list of Lonely Eagles on November 23, 2016, at the age of ninety-seven. His family scattered some of his ashes near Las Cruces on the family land he always called the Mesa. The family still owns part of the old homestead.

A few years before his death, he was asked how he wanted to be remembered. He paused a long time, considering the answer. He had saved lives, worked to integrate everything he possibly could, and spoken to school and community groups to share his view of history. Of course, he wanted to be known as a good doctor and a man who shattered barriers. But he decided there was something more important.

"As a good parent," he finally said. "Yeah, I think that's important for all Black parents. I agree with Obama's telling the folks that they have to be responsible for their kids. Remember me as a good surgeon and the best parent I knew how to be." That's why this story is not complete without a chapter on his children.

Brenda Joyce Williams had her own firsthand experiences with the pain of racism as a very young child. When the Williams family first moved to Chicago, they lived in an apartment outside of Hyde Park. Her Catholic parents enrolled her in a Catholic school, St. Thomas the Apostle in Hyde Park. She attended that school until third grade. Then Brenda remembers how, "after church one day, my parents were talking to Father and my dad being very upset when they came out. I guess at that time the school was becoming, in their view, too Black so . . . the Black kids who were not living in the parish couldn't go to the school anymore."

Her father responded by enrolling her in the

University of Chicago Laboratory School, one of Chicago's most exclusive private coed day schools. Even today, the Lab School is considered "the mothership of progressive education." Many of the students are children of university faculty and staff. Both Malia and Sasha Obama attended the Lab School until their father left Chicago for an out-of-town job.

Although Brenda thrived academically at school, she faced prejudice among some of her schoolmates. She can remember a girl saying, "You know, you remind me of my maid." Brenda also had kids ask her, "You, when are you going to take a bath? When are you going to, you know, wash your skin?"

She didn't tell her parents about these events. She worked to fit in, at least until adolescence, when acts of prejudice grew more subtle. She felt a growing distance from white friends, who were uninterested in social issues she cared passionately about. There were unwritten rules, parties she wasn't invited to, classmates who stopped talking to her. Kids started to separate racially and she began hanging out only with other Black kids.

Her behavior was truly foreign to her father, a man who spent his life promoting integration every chance he saw. His childhood had been one of exclusion by force. He found it difficult to understand why his daughter voluntarily segregated herself. After being a minority in every group event for so long, she found being surrounded by other Black youth empowering. "I guess I would be considered a Black nationalist or, you know, Black militant," Brenda admitted.

A growing social consciousness led her to attend civil rights and Black Power events in the late '60s, including a Black Panther Party rally. There she saw firsthand how a young Fred Hampton used his words and charisma to talk down a potentially violent confrontation.

The Black Panther Party for Self-Defense was a political party formed in 1966 by college students in Oakland, California. Fred Hampton, deputy chairman of the Illinois chapter, grew up in the Chicago suburb of Maywood. He excelled in high school and enrolled in a prelaw program at Triton Junior College after graduation. He was only twenty when he joined

Black Panther Fred Hampton testifies at a meeting on the death of two men in 1969.

the Black Panther Party and rapidly rose to a position of leadership.

Fred Hampton set up what were called survival programs in Illinois. Those including a free medical

258

clinic and a free breakfast program for schoolchildren. (The Black Panthers breakfast program helped inspire the national School Breakfast Program that began in 1975 and still feeds school-age children today.)

He also built a multiracial, multi-class coalition among groups, races, and organizations that would otherwise have been enemies. Coalition members participated in the survival programs and supported one another at protests, strikes, and demonstrations. For example, Fred Hampton and José Cha Cha Jiménez of the Young Lords (a Puerto Rican organization) were arrested twice in February 1969. Both men were charged with mob action for peacefully picketing at the Wicker Park Welfare Office in a protest over mistreatment of patrons.

The white media largely ignored the Black Panthers' survival programs and concentrated on reporting about their assertive style of protest, grim faces, and black leather jackets. They broadcast Fred Hampton's sometimes violent rhetoric about political empowerment. In his speeches, he said things like

"There have been many attacks made upon the Black Panther Party, so we feel it's best to be an armed propaganda unit. But the basic thing is to educate." City, police, and FBI officials focused on the armed part. Many community members understood the message about safety and what he was out to accomplish. The children involved in the breakfast program did not care much about politics. What mattered to them, and to their parents, were the eggs, meat, and cereal they were given to fill their stomachs before school.

Hampton's success at coalition building and mobilizing young people made him the focus of an FBI investigation just as Dr. Martin Luther King had been. On December 4, 1969, barely a year after Dr. King's assassination, Hampton was shot in his sleep by members of the Chicago police. He was only twenty-one.

Brenda Williams "always remembered what a true leader he was and the fact that he was murdered. I think of the Panther leaders that I [knew] . . . he might have been the strongest." She was obviously not neutral, but then, no one could be neutral about the man who appeared to define the term *young, gifted and Black*. A man who fought against the same unjust rules and worked for the same principles of health care and education her family did.

After graduating high school, Brenda attended Pomona College in Oakland, California. After graduation, she went to Ghana, in Africa, for a year to study West African literature. When she returned to the US, it was off to Boston for a master's degree from Boston University. Then she broke a color barrier on her own when she joined the all-white staff at the *Standard-Times* in New Bedford, Massachusetts. In 1980, Robert Maynard, the first Black editor and publisher of a mainstream newspaper, recruited her to work at the *Oakland Tribune*, taking her back to California.

Her writing life covered issues ranging from the United States War on Terror to the impact of racial discrimination on health. She has been published in the *New York Times* and in *Thinking Black: Some of the Nation's Best Black Columnists Speak Their Mind*, a 1996 anthology of African American columnists, under her married name, Brenda Payton Jones. She has also appeared on California's national public radio station.

Dr. James Buchanan Williams II was young enough to miss a lot of the turmoil in the 1960s. Memories of his father still influence the way he practices medicine today. He began accompanying his father on rounds and house calls when he was young. (Doctors used to visit patients at their homes, especially elderly patients or young children.) He joined his father on medical road trips, including visits to an Indiana hospital where Dr. Williams had privileges. Those trips always included a stop at Dairy Queen on the way home. And he first scrubbed in to observe his father during surgery at fifteen, years before Take Our Child to Work Day got started in 1993.

When he decided to become a doctor, he did his pre-med studies at Creighton University. He then returned to the Midwest, where he attended medical school at the University of Illinois. He received surgery training at the University of Minnesota. He became a colorectal surgeon after completing medical school. Like his father, he is a member of the National Medical Association and a Fellow of the American Academy of Surgeons. He still enjoys skiing and boating.

He remembers his father as one of the most heroic people he ever knew, and not just because of his actions during the war or skills in an operating room. "My father did not talk a lot about the Freeman Field incident. But he was always a strong believer in rights regardless of color. On any issue, if justice was not being served, my father was willing to stand up for what, or who, was right."

James Jr. also described how his father dealt with hospital employees. His father always paused to say "Bonjour" to St. Bernard's Haitian custodian and used the Spanish he learned in his youth in New Mexico to chat with the Mexican chef. He talked to the doctors and nurses exactly the same as he did to that janitor and the chef. He listened to his patients. He would touch a patient on the shoulder or knee. His son called it a healing touch and repeats the gesture with his own patients.

History overflows with stories of men and women who seem larger than life. We often look at them and their accomplishments in awe, assuming they had to have been special from birth. Dr. James Buchanan Williams produced one additional legacy. He showed that a hero can be anyone from anywhere. His daughter said about her father, "He didn't make out like he was a big hero, it was just that's what he had to do."

Look in the mirror. You will see someone capable of making all the difference in the world.

AFTERWORD

History of Black Medicine

BEFORE EUROPEANS TRAVELED TO Africa and enslaved large numbers of the population, many Africans possessed specialized math and science knowledge. For example, European travelers noted that the people of Fida, who lived on the coast of Benin, in western Africa, performed extensive calculations and kept exact accounts by memory as easily as Europeans did with pen and paper. According to one agent for the French Royal African Company in 1732:

> The Fidasians [on the coast of Benin, Africa] are
> so expert in keeping their accounts, that they
> easily reckon as exact, and as quick by memory,
> as we can do with pen and ink, though the sum
> amount to never so many thousands: which very

> *much facilitates the trade the Europeans have*
> *with them.*

This knowledge was frequently kept secret and passed only from parent to child. When experts were enslaved and sent across the ocean into slavery, their knowledge was stolen from their homeland. The slave trade kidnapped and enslaved an uncountable number of great minds from the African continent and left them to waste on a plantation or the bottom of the Atlantic Ocean.

The excellence exhibited by Clara Belle and Jasper Williams and their offspring was no accident. People who lived in long-ago Africa were skilled artisans, mathematicians, scientists, and doctors. Dreamers who looked at the sky and longed to fly were forced into hard labor in the New World. Those men and women did not lose their intelligence, skills, or dreams when they were stolen from Africa and brought across the ocean.

Even before emancipation, a number of Blacks accumulated the knowledge and skills to practice medicine in the US, many without formal medical school training. In 1783, James Derham became the first Black man to formally practice medicine in the US, although he never had a doctor's license. As a youth, he was enslaved to a Dr. John Kearsley and studied some of his owner's work. At fifteen, he was sold, and over the years, he went from one slaveholder to another. Several of his owners were doctors. While serving them, he seized opportunities to increase his practical medical knowledge. Eventually he was sold to New Orleans doctor Robert Dove. Recognizing the Black man's abilities, Dr. Dove made him an assistant and soon granted him his freedom. He even helped Derham open his own medical practice in New Orleans.

In 1837, James McCune Smith, a free man in New York City, became the first Black American to obtain a medical degree—one he had to travel to Scotland to acquire. He trained at the University of Glasgow Medical School and graduated near the top of his class.

Back in New York, Smith practiced at the Manhattan Colored Orphan Asylum until it was burned by a white mob during the July 1863 New York Draft Riot. Thousands of working-class New Yorkers rioted in Manhattan, protesting laws enacting a draft to send men off to fight in the ongoing Civil War. Some historians consider the riots among the bloodiest and most destructive in US history. Numerous Black people were lynched by the mobs, and a police officer was killed while trying to evacuate children from the Colored Orphan Asylum.

After the destruction of the orphan asylum, Dr. Smith became medical director for the newly opened Wilberforce University, the first college owned and operated by Black men. Although Smith's writings were published in many US medical journals, he was another Black doctor never admitted to the AMA. He used his knowledge and writing talent to refute racist misconceptions about the capabilities and intelligence of people of African descent, even debunking theories about Blacks found in Thomas Jefferson's *Notes on the State of Virginia*. Smith was an abolitionist and friend of Frederick Douglass. He contributed to

Douglass's newspaper and wrote the introduction to his book *My Bondage and My Freedom*.

George Washington Williams (no relation), the first Black member of the Ohio legislature, described the depth of racial prejudice he saw in post–Civil War America:

> *One of the standing arguments against the Negro was that he lacked the faculty of solving mathematical problems. This charge was made without a disposition to allow him an opportunity to submit himself to a proper test. It was equivalent to putting out a man's eyes, and then asserting boldly that he cannot see; of manacling his ankles, and charging him with the inability to run.*

Unfortunately, many race-based disparities in health care still exist. The National Medical Association continues its work in trying to counteract them in the twenty-first century. Black Americans have gained better access to health care, and the

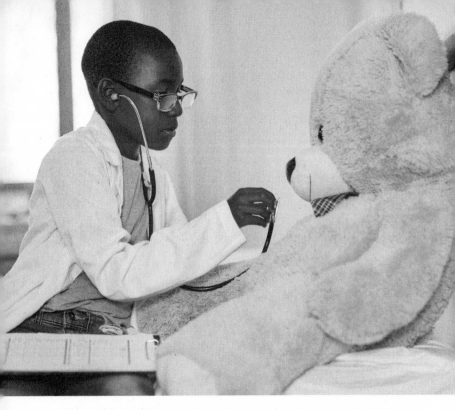

So much has changed. You, too, can follow your dreams, just as the Williams brothers did.

professional staffs and patient populations at hospitals are desegregated.

African American physicians are no longer limited. We just need more of them. They still face many challenges their white counterparts do not. Dr. Williams noted in 2000 that "we still have people at some hospitals who say they would never train any Blacks in specialties such as, for example, surgery. Today that exists."

The number of Black medical schools in the United States jumped from two to four with the addition of the Los Angeles Charles R. Drew University of Medicine and Science in 1966 and Morehouse School of Medicine in 1975. Even with those additions, only about 5 percent of US doctors and only 7 percent of medical students are Black, according to information from the Student National Medical Association. Some people still believe Black physicians did not really earn their medical degrees and did not put in the hard work and dedication exemplified by the people in this story. The Williams brothers stand as proof they are wrong.

BIBLIOGRAPHY

"Ace Negro Flier Takes Command of 477th Group at Godman Field." *The Courier-Journal* (Louisville, KY.), June 22, 1945, p. 9.

Afedruru, Lominda. "Clubfoot: Why it happens and how doctors treat it." *Daily Monitor*, Feb. 15, 2021. https://www.monitor.co.ug/uganda/magazines /healthy-living/clubfoot-why-it-happens-and-how-doctors-treat-it-3291794.

Allen, L. C. "The Negro Health Problem: Read before the General Sessions, American Public Health Association." *The American Journal of Public Health*, Jacksonville, FL., Nov. 30–Dec. 4, 1914, pp. 194–203.

"Anderson, Charles Alfred 'Chief': Father of African American Aviation /Pilot." National Aviation Hall of Fame. https://www.nationalaviation .org/our-enshrinees/anderson-charles-alfred/.

"Anti-Lynching Legislation Renewed." History, Art & Archives: US House of Representatives. https://history.house.gov/Exhibitions-and -Publications/BAIC/Historical-Essays/Temporary-Farewell /Anti-Lynching-Legislation/.

Barbot, John, and Claes Rålamb. "A Description of the Coasts of North and South-Guinea; and of Ethiopia Inferior, *vulgarly* Angola [. . .] And a New Relation of the Province of *Guiana*, and of the great Rivers of *Amazons* and *Oronoque* in South-America. With an Appendix being a General Account of the First Discoveries of *America*, in the fourteenth Century, and some Observations thereon. And a Geographical, Political, and Natural History of the *Antilles*-Islands, in the North-Sea of America." [London], 1732, p. 339. https://catalog.princeton.edu/ catalog/9972902243506421#view.

Becton Jr., Gen. Julius. The HistoryMakers Digital Archive, interviewed by Larry Crowe, Aug. 27, 2012. https://thehistorymakers.org.

Blackburn, Piper Hudspeth. "How Racism Shaped the Public Health Response to the 1918 Spanish Flu Pandemic." Northwestern University, May 3, 2020. https://nationalsecurityzone.medill .northwestern.edu/covidanalyzer/news/how-racism-colored-the-public -health-response-to-the-1918-spanish-flu-pandemic/.

Brown, DeNeen L. "A Black WWII veteran was beaten and blinded, fueling the civil rights movement." *Washington Post*, Mar. 31, 2021.

https://www.washingtonpost.com/history/2021/03/31
/isaac-woodard-truman-integration-military/.

Bush, George W. "Remarks on Presenting the Congressional Gold Medal
to the Tuskegee Airmen." Government Publishing Office, Mar. 29,
2007. https://www.govinfo.gov/content/pkg/WCPD-2007-04-02/html
/WCPD-2007-04-02-Pg387-3.htm.

"Call for Military Memorabilia: The Tuskegee Airmen and Lockbourne."
Ohio History Connection, Feb. 12, 2016. https://www.ohiohistory
.org/learn/collections/history/history-blog/2016/february-2016
/call-for-military-memorabilia-the-tuskegee-airmen.

Chappell, Roy. The HistoryMakers Digital Archive, interviewed by Larry
Crowe, May 14, 2002. https://thehistorymakers.org.

"Children's Crusade." National Museum of African American History &
Culture. https://nmaahc.si.edu/blog/childrens-crusade.

Clark, James. "The Tragic and Ignored History of Black Veterans." *Task &
Purpose*, Dec. 9, 2016. https://taskandpurpose.com/history
/tragic-ignored-history-black-veterans/.

Cobb, W. Montague. "The President-Elect." *Journal of the National Medical
Association*, Nov. 1974, vol. 66.

Davis, F. James. *Who Is Black? One Nation's Definition*. University Park,
PA: Penn State University Press, 1991.

Davis, Rick. "The Fight for Equality." *Creighton University
Magazine*, Summer 2000. https://dspace2.creighton.edu/xmlui
/handle/10504/110452.

"Discussion with Clara Belle Williams and family." NMSU Library, May 10,
1980, video, https://www.youtube.com/watch?v=kIfy_rI-fKs.

District Court Eastern District of South Carolina. "Dissenting opinion
in *Harry Briggs, Jr., et al.* v. *R. W. Elliott, Chairman, et al.*" National
Archives and Records Administration: Records of District Courts
of the United States, 1865–1902, filed June 23, 1951.https://catalog
.archives.gov/id/279306.

Du Bois, W. E. B. "Returning Soldiers." *The Crisis*, May 1919, vol. 18, no. 1.
https://glc.yale.edu/returning-soldiers.

Durr, Eric. "'Rainbow Division' that represented the United States formed in
New York in August 1917." US Army, July 24, 2017. https://www

.army.mil/article/191270/rainbow_division_that_represented_the
_united_states_formed_in_new_york_in_august_1917.

EJI Staff. "Lynching in America: Targeting Black Veterans." Equal Justice
Initiative, 2017. https://eji.org/wp-content/uploads/2019/10/lynching
-in-america-targeting-black-veterans-web.pdf.

"Employment of Negro Man Power in War." Army War College, Office
of the Commandant, Oct. 1925. https://www.fdrlibrary.org
/documents/356632/390886/tusk_doc_a.pdf.

Flexner, Abraham. "Medical Education in the United States and Canada."
Carnegie Foundation for the Advancement of Teaching (New
York, 1910), Bulletin No. 4. http://archive.carnegiefoundation.org
/publications/pdfs/elibrary/Carnegie_Flexner_Report.pdf.

"Flying Black Medics." *Ebony* magazine, June 1970, vol. 25, no. 8.

"Flying Black Medics Dramatize Cairo's Poor Health Care." *Jet* magazine,
Mar. 5, 1970.

Francis, Megan Ming. *Civil Rights and the Making of the Modern
American State.* New York: Cambridge University Press, 2014.

Fujimura, Sara Francis. "Purple Death: The Great Flu of 1918." *Perspectives
in Health: The Magazine of the Pan American Health Organization,*
Nov. 3, 2003, vol. 8, no. 3. https://www3.paho.org/English/DD/PIN
/Number18_article5.htm.

Gamble, Vanessa N. "'There Wasn't a Lot of Comforts in Those Days':
African Americans, Public Health, and the 1918 Influenza Epidemic."
Public Health Reports. 2010; 125 (Suppl. 3):114–122. https://www
.ncbi.nlm.nih.gov/pmc/articles/PMC2862340/.

Gómez, Félix Disla. "Mocano Esteban Hotesse Pacheco será
reconocido por universidad en Estados Unidos." *Diariolibre,*
Aug. 22, 2018. https://www.diariolibre.com/revista/cultura
/mocano-esteban-hotesse-pacheco-sera-reconocido-por-universidad-en
-estados-unidos-DH10609912.

Guzmán, Will. "Border Physician: The Life of Lawrence A. Nixon, 1883–
1966." *Open Access Theses & Dissertations,* 2010. https://scholarworks
.utep.edu/open_etd/2495.

Hankins, Michael. "Mutiny at Freeman Field: The Tuskegee Airmen on Trial,
Part 2." Smithsonian National Air and Space Museum, June 9, 2020.

https://airandspace.si.edu/stories/editorial
/mutiny-freeman-field-tuskegee-airmen-trial-part-2.

Haulman, Daniel L. "A Tale of Two Commanders." *Air Power History*,
Summer 2018, vol. 65, no. 2. https://www.jstor.org/stable/26571113.

Hennessy-Fiske, Molly. "Airmen Plan to Attend Inauguration." *Los Angeles
Times*, Jan. 18, 2009. https://www.newspapers.com/clip/37178064
/roger-c-terry/.

Higginbotham, Mitchell L. "Mitchell L. Higginbotham Collection
(AFC/2001/001/18255)." Veterans History Project, American
Folklife Center, Library of Congress, interviewed by Mary Crowl,
audio, May 2003. http://memory.loc.gov/diglib/vhp/bib/loc.natlib
.afc2001001.18255.

Higgins, Abigail. "Red Summer of 1919: How Black WWI Vets Fought
Back Against Racist Mobs." History.com, July 26, 2019. https://www
.history.com/news/red-summer-1919-riots-chicago-dc-great-migration.

History.com editors. "Ku Klux Klan." History.com: A&E Television
Networks, Oct. 29, 2009. http://history.com/topics/reconstruction
/ku-klux-klan.

History.com editors. "Plessy v. Ferguson." History.com: A&E Television
Networks, Oct. 29, 2009. https://www.history.com/topics
/black-history/plessy-v-ferguson.

History.com editors. "Police kill two members of the Black
Panther Party." History.com: A&E Television Networks,
Nov. 13, 2009. https://www.history.com/this-day-in-history
/police-kill-two-members-of-the-black-panther-party.

"History of the Imhotep National Conference on Hospital Integration."
Journal of the National Medical Association, Jan. 1962, vol. 54, no. 1.

Homan, Lynn M. and Thomas Reilly. *Black Knights: The Story of the
Tuskegee Airmen*. Gretna, LA: Pelican Publishing Company, Jan.
2001.

"Influenza Pandemic." University Libraries: University of Washington.
https://content.lib.washington.edu/exhibits/WWI/influenza.html.

Johnson, Ernest E. "Negro Fliers Seen Victims of General's Planned
Segregation." *Pittsburgh Courier* (Pittsburgh, PA), June 2, 1945.

Johnson, James Weldon. "The Riots." *The Crisis*, Sept. 1919, vol. 18, no. 5.

Jones, Brenda Payton. The HistoryMakers Digital Archive, interviewed by Loretta Henry, Apr. 3, 2006. https://thehistorymakers.org.

"Judge Lynch at Cameron." *Marshall Messenger* (Marshall, TX), Nov. 8, 1907.

Kennedy, John F. "Civil Rights Announcement, 1963." *American Experience*, June 11, 1963. https://www.pbs.org/wgbh /americanexperience/features/jfk-civilrights/.

King, Gilbert. "Remembering Henry Johnson, the Soldier Called Black Death." *Smithsonian Magazine*, Oct. 25, 2011. https://www .smithsonianmag.com/history/remembering-henry -johnson-the-soldier-called-black-death-117386701/.

Klein, Linda. "'Grandma,' 3 Sons Run Clinic—Her Dream Come True." *Chicago Tribune* (Chicago, IL), June 27, 1964.

Knox III, George Levi. The HistoryMakers Digital Archive, interviewed by Larry Crowe, Mar. 29, 2005. https://thehistorymakers.org.

Lamb, Chris. "The police beating that opened America's eyes to Jim Crow's brutality." *The Conversation*, Feb. 11, 2016. https://theconversation .com/the-police-beating-that-opened-americas-eyes-to-jim-crows -brutality-53932.

Lantigua-Williams, Juleyka. "An Unknown Latino Tuskegee Airman Has Been Discovered." *The Atlantic*, Nov. 5, 2015. https://www.theatlantic.com /politics/archive/2015/11/unknown-latino-tuskegee-airman-discovered /433479/.

Little, Hiram. The HistoryMakers Digital Archive, interviewed by Denise Gines, Sept. 10, 2007. https://thehistorymakers.org.

"Longview Wakes to Fighting and Riots among the White and Black." *Marshall Messenger* (Marshall, TX), July 15, 1919. http://www .lynchingintexas.org/items/show/30.

Lynching in Texas Staff. "Lynching of Alex Johnson." *Lynching in Texas*, Feb. 14, 2018. http://www.lynchingintexas.org/items/show/84.

MacGregor, Morris J. "Defense Studies—Integration of the Armed Forces, 1940–1965." Center of Military History, United States Army (Washington, DC, 1981). https://history.army.mil/html/books/050/50 -1-1/cmhPub_50-1-1.pdf.

Markoutsas, Elaine. "Pioneer Clara Williams, 95: Model Mother to Generations." *Chicago Tribune*, May 10, 1981.

Military Wiki. "Mariano Goybet: 1918 Victory With the Red Hand: African American soldiers in the battle." Military Wikia, retrieved Jan. 10, 2021. https://military.wikia.org/wiki/Mariano_Goybet#1918_victory _With_the_Red_Hand:_African_American_soldiers_in_the_battle.

Moody, Terry, and Clarence Fielder. "The African American Experience in Southern New Mexico." New Mexico History: State Records Center & Archives, 2000. https://newmexicohistory.org/2000/10/29 /african-american-experience-in-southern-new-mexico/.

Morris, Walter. "Walter Morris Collection (AFC/2001/001/02946)." Veterans History Project, American Folklife Center, Library of Congress, interviewed by Judith Kent, audio file, Nov. 2002. http://memory.loc .gov/diglib/vhp/bib/loc.natlib.afc2001001.02946.

Murphy, Major John D. "The Freeman Field Mutiny: A Study in Leadership" (A Research Paper Presented to the Research Department Air Command and Staff College in Partial Fulfillment of the Graduation Requirements of ACSC, March 1997). https://apps.dtic.mil/sti/pdfs /ADA397891.pdf.

National Medical Association website, accessed Dec. 3, 2020. https://www .nmanet.org/.

"New Deal at Godman." *The Journal and Guide*, June 23, 1945, Home Edition, vol. XLVI, no. 25.

"Nip It in the Bud." *True Democrat* (St. Francisville, LA), Dec. 21, 1918, p. 2.

Obama, Barack. "President Barack Obama's Inaugural Address." White House: President Barack Obama, Jan. 21, 2009. https://obamawhitehouse .archives.gov/blog/2009/01/21/president-barack-obamas-inaugural-address.

"Ohio Capital Opposes Transfer of 477th Pilots." *The Chicago Defender* (Chicago, IL), Feb. 9, 1946.

Ortiz, Erik. "Racial violence and a pandemic: How the Red Summer of 1919 relates to 2020." NBC News, June 21, 2020. https://www.nbcnews .com/news/us-news/racial-violence-pandemic-how-red-summer-1919 -relates-2020-n1231499.

Payton, Brenda. "Payton: Thinking of Tuskegee Airman Father during Black History Month." *The Mercury News* (San Jose, CA), Feb. 2014.

Payton, Brenda. "Tuskegee Airmen Finally Receive Their Recognition." *East Bay Times* (San Francisco Bay Area), Apr. 3, 2007.

Perl, Peter. "Nation's Capital Held at Mercy of the Mob." *Washington Post*, July 16, 1989. https://www.washingtonpost.com/archive /lifestyle/magazine/1989/07/16/nations-capital-held-at-mercy-of-the -mob/89f8f5bc-7e32-43aa-8479-d1213768e769/.

Poletika, Nicole. "Blacks Must Wage Two Wars: The Freeman Field Uprising & WWII Desegregation." *Indiana History Blog*, July 31, 2017. https:// blog.history.in.gov/blacks-must-wage-two-wars-the-freeman-field -uprising-wwii-desegregation/.

Ramirez, Steve. "Dr. James Williams, Las Crucen Who Served with Tuskegee Airmen, Dies." *Las Cruces Sun News* (Las Cruces, NM), Nov. 27, 2016.

"Red Summer: The Race Riots of 1919." National WWI Museum and Memorial. https://www.theworldwar.org/learn/wwi/red-summer.

Roosevelt, Eleanor. "My Day." The Eleanor Roosevelt Papers Digital Edition, Dec. 5, 1956. https://www2.gwu.edu/~erpapers/myday /displaydocedits.cfm?_y=1956&_f=md003660.

Roosevelt, Jr., Theodore. *Rank and File: True Stories of the Great War*. New York: C. Scribner's Sons, Jan. 1, 1928.

Roughton, Randy. "Black Airmen turn racism, bigotry, into opportunity." Air Force News Service, Feb. 4, 2014. https:// www.af.mil/News/Article-Display/Article/473251 /black-airmen-turn-racism-bigotry-into-opportunity/.

Schilter-Lowe, Merrie. "Tuskegee Airmen knew true meaning of sacrifice." *Daily Republic* (Fairfield-Suisun City, CA), Nov. 26, 2018. https:// www.dailyrepublic.com/all-dr-news/solano-news/military /tuskegee-airmen-knew-true-meaning-of-sacrifice/.

Scott, Lawrence P., and William M. Womack, Sr. *Double V: The Civil Rights Struggle of the Tuskegee Airmen*. East Lansing: Michigan State University Press, Aug. 1, 1994.

"Separate Cars for the Races." *Weekly Messenger* (St. Martins, LA), May 23, 1896, vol. XI, no. 15. https://chroniclingamerica.loc.gov/lccn /sn88064454/1896-05-23/ed-1/seq-1/.

Smith, David A. The HistoryMakers Digital Archive, interviewed by Shawn Wilson, Apr. 19, 2006. https://thehistorymakers.org.

Smith, Quentin. "Quentin Smith Collection, (AFC/2001/001/03001)." Veterans History Project, American Folklife Center, Library of

Congress, interviewed by Timothy Sanders, July 2002, audio file.
https://memory.loc.gov/diglib/vhp/bib/loc.natlib.afc2001001.03001.

"'Standards, No Compromise': a 75-year profile of the Army's Officer
Candidate School." *Army Times*, Mar. 15, 2017. https://www
.armytimes.com/army-times/2017/03/15/standards-no-compromise-a
-75-year-profile-of-the-armys-officer-candidate-school/.

Starkey, J. J. "Pioneer History: Fighting Apache Indians." *Kerrville Times*
(Kerrville, TX), Oct. 19, 1933, p. 4.

Stevens, John D. "From the Back of the Foxhole: Black Correspondents in
World War II." *Journalism Monographs*, Feb. 1973, no. 27. http://files
.eric.ed.gov/fulltext/ED096675.pdf.

Stockley, Grif. "Elaine Massacre 1919." *Encyclopedia of Arkansas*. https://
encyclopediaofarkansas.net/entries/elaine-massacre-of-1919-1102/.

Terry, Roger. "Eyewitness to Jim Crow, Roger 'Bill' Terry Remembers."
PBS: Jim Crow History. https://web.archive.org/web/20051027032849
/http://www.jimcrowhistory.org/resources/narratives/Roger_Terry.htm.

Thompson, Carolyn. "Tuskegee Airmen Receive Congressional Gold
Medal." AP News, Nov. 11, 2016. https://apnews.com/article/6a71f4986
4f546f188d43aeb605bc5c7.

Thompson, James G. "Should I Sacrifice to Live 'Half-American'?"
Pittsburgh Courier (Pittsburgh, PA), Letter to the Editor, Jan. 31, 1942.

"Tribute to Air Force 2nd Lieutenant Esteban Hotesse, Tuskegee Airman,
Dominican-American." *Congressional Record*, Mar. 2, 2016, vol. 162,
no. 34. https://www.govinfo.gov/content/pkg/CREC-2016-03-02/html
/CREC-2016-03-02-pt1-PgE264-3.htm.

"Tuskegee Airmen Still Flying High." *Ebony* magazine, Nov. 1994, vol. 50, no. 1.

Tuskegee Airmen Inc. website http://tuskegeeairmen.org/.

Uenuma, Francine. "The Massacre of Black Sharecroppers That Led the
Supreme Court to Curb the Racial Disparities of the Justice System."
Smithsonian Magazine, Aug. 2, 2018. https://www.smithsonianmag
.com/history/death-hundreds-elaine-massacre-led-supreme-court-take
-major-step-toward-equal-justice-african-americans-180969863/.

United States Congress Senate. "Anti-Lynching Bill." Senate Reports (7951),
67th Congress: 2nd Session, 1921–22, July 28, 1922, vol. 2,

pp. 33–34 bill, July 28, 1922. https://documents.alexanderstreet
.com/d/1002913442.

United States Supreme Court. *"Brown v. Board of Education,"* National
Archives and Records Administration: Records of the Supreme Court
of the United States, 1772–2007, decided: May 17, 1954. https://catalog
.archives.gov/id/1656510.

United States Supreme Court. *"Nixon v. Herndon et al.,"* National Archives
and Records Administration: Records of the Supreme Court of the
United States, 1772–2007, decided: Mar. 7, 1927. https://catalog
.archives.gov/id/126750941.

United States Supreme Court. *"Plessy v. Ferguson,"* National Archives and
Records Administration: Records of the Supreme Court of the United
States, 1772–2007, decided: May 18, 1896. https://catalog.archives.gov
/id/1685178.

Vedantam, Shankar, Maggie Penman, Jennifer Schmidt, Chloe Connelly,
and Tara Boyle. "Remembering Anarcha, Lucy, and Betsey: The
Mothers of Modern Gynecology." *NPR Hidden Brain*, Feb. 7, 2017,
audio file. https://www.npr.org/2017/02/07/513764158/remembering
-anarcha-lucy-and-betsey-the-mothers-of-modern-gynecology.

Wallace, George C., "Inaugural Address of Governor George C. Wallace."
Alabama Department of Archives and History, Jan. 14, 1963. https://
digital.archives.alabama.gov/digital/collection/voices/id/2952.

Warren, James C., Lt. Col. USAF. *The Freeman Field Mutiny*. San Rafael,
CA: Donna Ewald, Publisher, 1995.

Washington, Harriet A. "Apology Shines Light on Racial Schism in
Medicine." *New York Times*, Essay July 29, 2008. https://www
.nytimes.com/2008/07/29/health/views/29essa.html.

Weekley, Rachel Franklin. "A strong pull, a long pull, and a pull altogether,
Topeka's contribution to the campaign for school desegregation."
National Park Service: US Department of the Interior, Jan. 24, 2001.
http://npshistory.com/publications/brvb/hrs.pdf.

Welles, Orson. "Commentary: Affidavit of Isaac Woodard." July 28, 1946,
audio file. https://www.youtube.com/watch?v=P11sW1sXNbs.

"What God Hath Wrought." *Journal of the National Medical Association*,
Editorial, 1968, vol. 60, no.6, pp. 518–521.

Whayne, Jeannie M. "Low Villains and Wickedness in High Places: Race and Class in the Elaine Riots." *The Arkansas Historical Quarterly*, Autumn 1999, vol. 58, no. 3. https://doi.org/10.2307/40026231.

Williams, George Washington. *History of the Negro Race in America from 1619 to 1880*. New York: G. P. Putnam's Sons, 1883, Vol 1.

Williams, Dr. James B., The HistoryMakers Digital Archive, interviewed by Larry Crowe, July 16, 2008. https://thehistorymakers.org.

Wolf, Ronald W. "Black History Month: Stay Focused! Stick to It! Get It Done!" US Army, Feb. 25, 2020. https://www.army.mil/article/233012/black_history_month_stay_focused_stick_to_it_get_it_done.

Wood, Ted. "Citizen Editor Promises to Print Record of 477th as Community Protests Article Slurring Outfis [sic]," *Ohio State News* (Columbus, OH), Feb. 2, 1946. https://digital-collections.columbuslibrary.org/digital/collection/african/id/2591.

Wormser, Richard. *Red Summer* (1919). WNET group, accessed Feb. 2021. https://www.thirteen.org/wnet/jimcrow/stories_events_red.html.

ADDITIONAL RESOURCES FOR YOUR ENJOYMENT

Double Victory: The Tuskegee Airmen at War. Lucasfilm documentary, narrated by Cuba Gooding Jr. https://www.youtube.com/watch?v=QmcpILi1Rxc.

Taveras, Emely. "Esteban Hotesse dominicano que perteneció al grupo Tuskegee en la segunda guerra mundial | La Bio." Oct. 16, 2020. https://www.youtube .com/watch?v=fheFccZB0fg.

The Triple Nickels World War II—555th Training Exercises video. Jan. 4, 2010. https://www.youtube.com /watch?v=Il5E0TrG_eU.

The Tuskegee Airmen, They Fought Two Wars. PBS video, produced and directed by W. Drew Perkins and Bill Reifenberger, narrated by Ossie Davis.

In addition to the Tuskegee Airman from the Dominican Republic, another member of the famed group had Chinese ancestry:

Strain, Daniel. "Her father was a Tuskegee Airman. She's sharing his legacy." University of Colorado, Feb. 2021. https://www.colorado.edu/today/2021/02/25 /her-father-was-tuskegee-airman-shes-sharing-his-legacy.

SOURCE NOTES

Chapter 1: Meet JB Williams

"The newspapers deemed . . .": "Judge Lynch at Cameron" *Marshall Messenger* (Marshall, TX), Nov. 8, 1907.

"driving, ambitious man . . . with society.": Elaine Markoutsas, "Pioneer Clara Williams, 95: Model Mother to Generations," *Chicago Tribune,* May 10, 1981.

"as a child she sometimes leaned . . .": "Discussion with Clara Belle Williams and family," NMSU Library, May 10, 1980, video, https:// www.youtube.com/watch?v=kIfy_rI-fKs.

"This is . . . my little schoolteacher.": Markoutsas, Pioneer Clara Williams, 95.

"He and Dr. Nixon . . . left his home.": Dr. James B. Williams, "Dr. James Williams describes his father's civil rights activities," TheHistoryMakers Digital Archive, interviewed by Larry Crowe, July 16, 2008, Session 1, Tape 1, Story 6, https://thehistorymakers.org.

Chapter 2: World War I

"He warned . . . rights must be respected.'": EJI Staff, "Lynching in America: Targeting Black Veterans," Equal Justice Initiative, 2017, 25, https://eji .org/wp-content/uploads/2019/10/lynching-in-america-targeting-black -veterans-web.pdf.

"Don't let it be said . . .": Piper Hudspeth Blackburn, "How Racism Shaped the Public Health Response to the 1918 Spanish Flu Pandemic," Northwestern University, May 3, 2020, https://nationalsecurityzone. medill.northwestern.edu/covidanalyzer/news/how-racism-colored-the-public-health-response-to-the-1918-spanish-flu-pandemic/.

"At the same time . . .": Vanessa N. Gamble, "'There Wasn't a Lot of Comforts in Those Days': African Americans, Public Health, and the 1918 Influenza Epidemic," *Public Health Reports,* 2010; 125 (Suppl. 3):114–122, https://www.ncbi.nlm.nih.gov/pmc/articles/ PMC2862340/.

"Theodore Roosevelt Jr. called . . .": Theodore Roosevelt Jr., *Rank and File: True Stories of the Great War,* New York: C. Scribner's Sons, Jan. 1, 1928.

"When they applied to join . . .": Eric Durr, "'Rainbow Division' that represented the United States formed in New York in August 1917," US Army, July 24, 2017, https://www.army.mil/article/191270 /rainbow_division_that_represented_the_united_states_formed_in _new_york_in_august_1917.

"Private Henry Johnson stood . . .": Gilbert King, "Remembering Henry Johnson, the Soldier Called 'Black Death,'" *Smithsonian Magazine*, Oct. 25, 2011, https://www.smithsonianmag.com/history /remembering-henry-johnson-the-soldier-called-black-death-117386701/.

"Each slash meant . . . let me tell you": ibid.

"There wasn't anything so fine . . .": ibid.

"In fact, after . . . leadership.": "Employment of Negro Man Power in War," Army War College, Office of the Commandant, Oct. 1925, https:// www.fdrlibrary.org/documents/356632/390886/tusk_doc_a.pdf.

Chapter 3: The Red Summer of 1919

"World War I was . . .": Abigail Higgins, "Red Summer of 1919: How Black WWI Vets Fought Back Against Racist Mobs," History.com, July 26, 2019, https:// www.history.com/news/red-summer-1919-riots-chicago-dc-great -migration.

"We are cowards and . . . the reason why.": W. E. B. Du Bois, "Returning Soldiers," *The Crisis*, May 1919, 13, https://glc.yale.edu/returning -soldiers.

"While they were overseas . . . all to see.": James Clark, "The Tragic and Ignored History of Black Veterans," Dec. 9, 2016, https:// taskandpurpose.com/history/tragic-ignored-history-black-veterans/.

"the problem was . . .": "Nip It in the Bud," *True Democrat* (St. Francisville, LA), Dec. 21, 1918, 2.

"A group of Black men . . . paid off.": Megan Ming Francis, *Civil Rights and the Making of the Modern American State*, Cambridge University Press, 2014.

"The governor of Arkansas . . . surrender immediately.": Jeannie M. Whayne, "Low Villains and Wickedness in High Places: Race and Class in the Elaine Riots," *The Arkansas Historical Quarterly*, Autumn 1999, vol. 58, no. 3, 285–313, https://doi.org/10.2307/40026231.

"under order to shoot . . .": Francine Uenuma, "The Massacre of Black Sharecroppers That Led the Supreme Court to Curb the Racial Disparities of the Justice System," *Smithsonian Magazine*,

Aug. 2, 2018, https://www.smithsonianmag.com/history/death-hundreds-elaine-massacre-led-supreme-court-take-major-step-toward-equal-justice-african-americans-180969863/.

"A seven-man committee . . . Arkansas had failed to do so": ibid.

"Many immigrants who . . . any other racist organization.": "Red Summer: The Race Riots of 1919," National WWI Museum and Memorial, https://www.theworldwar.org/learn/wwi/red-summer.

"Trouble began in Washington . . ." Peter Perl, "Nation's Capital Held at Mercy of the Mob," *Washington Post*, July 16, 1989, https://www.washingtonpost.com/archive/lifestyle/magazine/1989/07/16/nations-capital-held-at-mercy-of-the-mob/89f8f5bc-7e32-43aa-8479-d1213768e769/.

"They had . . . myself.": ibid.

"I knew . . . the White House.": James Weldon Johnson, "The Riots," *The Crisis*, Sept. 1919, vol. 18, no. 5, 241–244.

"Sensing the failure . . .": Abigail Higgins, "Red Summer of 1919: How Black WWI Vets Fought Back Against Racist Mobs," History.com, July 26, 2019, https://www.history.com/news/red-summer-1919-riots-chicago-dc-great-migration.

"General Goybet had no problem . . .": Military Wiki, "Mariano Goybet: 1918 Victory With the Red Hand: African American soldiers in the battle," accessed Jan. 10, 2021, https://military.wikia.org/wiki/Mariano_Goybet#1918_victory_With_the_Red_Hand:_African_American_soldiers_in_the_battle.

"There had been no trouble . . .": Grif Stockley, "Elaine Massacre 1919," *Encyclopedia of Arkansas*, https://encyclopediaofarkansas.net/entries/elaine-massacre-of-1919-1102/.

"The Washington riot . . . from me.": Richard Wormser, *Red Summer*, (1919), WNET Group, accessed Feb. 2021, https://www.thirteen.org/wnet/jimcrow/stories_events_red.html.

"One of those . . . *Chicago Defender*.": "Longview Wakes to Fighting and Riots Among the White and Black," *Marshall Messenger* (Marshall, TX), July 15, 1919, http://www.lynchingintexas.org/items/show/30.

"That included supporting . . .": "Anti-Lynching Legislation Renewed," History, Art & Archives: US House of Representatives, https://history.house.gov/Exhibitions-and-Publications/BAIC/Historical-Essays/Temporary-Farewell/Anti-Lynching-Legislation/.

Chapter 4: Starting a New Life

"This particular law stated . . .": Will Guzmán, "Border Physician: The Life of Lawrence A. Nixon, 1883–1966," *Open Access Theses & Dissertations*, 2010, 135, https://scholarworks.utep.edu/open_etd/2495.

"Although Dr. Nixon . . . the United States Constitution.": United States Supreme Court, "*Nixon v. Herndon et al.*," National Archives and Records Administration: Records of the Supreme Court of the United States, 1772–2007, decided: Mar. 7, 1927, https://catalog.archives.gov /id/126750941.

"[I]n the opinion . . . of African descent.": Terry Moody and Clarence Fielder, "The African-American Experience in Southern New Mexico," 2000, New Mexico History: State Records Center & Archives, https://newmexicohistory.org/2000/10/29 /african-american-experience-in-southern-new-mexico/.

"Jasper Fleming once described . . .": "Discussion with Clara Belle Williams and family," NMSU Library, May 10, 1980, video, https://www .youtube.com/watch?v=kIfy_rI-fKs.

"The local Black church . . .": Moody and Fielder, "The African American Experience."

"When the school superintendent . . .": "Discussion with Clara Belle Williams."

"Years later, the Williams . . .": "Discussion with Clara Belle Williams.

"The tendons around his feet . . .": Lominda Afedruru, "Clubfoot: Why it happens and how doctors treat it," *Daily Monitor*, Feb. 15, 2021, https://www.monitor.co.ug/uganda/magazines/healthy-living /clubfoot-why-it-happens-and-how-doctors-treat-it-3291794.

Chapter 5: Separate but Equal: *Plessy v. Ferguson*

"People who never grew . . . 1920s and 30s.": Randy Roughton, "Black Airmen turn racism, bigotry, into opportunity," Air Force News Service, Feb. 4, 2014, https://www.af.mil/News/Article-Display /Article/473251/black-airmen-turn-racism-bigotry-into-opportunity/.

"The Louisiana state law . . .": F. James Davis, *Who Is Black? One Nation's Definition*, University Park, PA: Penn State University Press, 1991.

"The problem, the justices . . .": United States Supreme Court, "*Plessy v. Ferguson*," National Archives and Records Administration: Records of the Supreme Court of the United States, 1772–2007, decided: May 18, 1896, https://catalog.archives.gov/id/1685178.

"According to an article . . .": "Separate Cars for the Races," *Weekly Messenger* (St. Martins, LA), May 23, 1896, vol. XI, no. 15, https://chroniclingamerica.loc.gov/lccn/sn88064454/1896-05-23/ed-1/seq-1/.

"According to Saje Mathieu . . .": Erik Ortiz, "Racial Violence and a Pandemic: How the Red Summer of 1919 Relates to 2020," NBC News, June 21, 2020, https://www.nbcnews.com/news/us-news/racial-violence-pandemic-how-red-summer-1919-relates-2020-n1231499.

Chapter 6: Growing Up JB

"She began by . . . crippled anymore.": Elaine Markoutsas, "Pioneer Clara Williams, 95: Model Mother to Generations," *Chicago Tribune*, May 10, 1981.

"JB never had a favorite . . .": Dr. James B. Williams, "Dr. James Williams lists his favorites," The HistoryMakers Digital Archive, interviewed by Larry Crowe, July 16, 2008, Session 1, Tape 1, Story 2, https://thehistorymakers.org.

"JB learned to shoot . . .": Dr. James B. Williams, "Dr. James Williams remembers the doctor who treated his brother's clubfoot," The HistoryMakers Digital Archive, interviewed by Larry Crowe, July 16, 2008, Session 1, Tape 2, Story 3, https://thehistorymakers.org.

"Victorio was chief of the Chihenne . . .": J. J. Starkey, "Pioneer History: Fighting Apache Indians," *Kerrville Times* (Kerrville, TX), Oct. 19, 1933, 4.

"He protected us, you know . . .": Dr. James B. Williams, "Dr. James Williams recalls his family's dog," The HistoryMakers Digital Archive, interviewed by Larry Crowe, July 16, 2008, Session 1, Tape 2, Story 2, https://thehistorymakers.org.

"JB was sure he knew . . .": ibid.

"You can do whatever . . .": "Discussion with Clara Belle Williams and family," NMSU Library, May 10, 1980, video, https://www.youtube.com/watch?v=kIfy_rI-fKs.

Chapter 7: Double V for Victory

"Private Jasper Williams . . . candidate group.": W. Montague Cobb, "The President-Elect," *Journal of the National Medical Association*, Nov. 1974, vol. 66, 519–524.

"At one point during WWII . . . (Officer Training School).": "'Standards, No Compromise', Army Times, Mar. 15, 2017, https://www.armytimes.com/army-times/2017/03/15/standards-no-compromise-a-75-year-profile-of-the-armys-officer-candidate-school/.

"Inside OCS we were . . ." Gen. Julius Becton Jr., "Julius Becton talks about attending Officer Candidate School in 1944," The HistoryMakers Digital Archive, interviewed by Larry Crowe, August 27, 2012, Session 1, Tape 3, Story 8, https://thehistorymakers.org.

"Being an American . . .": James G. Thompson, "Should I Sacrifice to Live 'Half-American'?", *Pittsburgh Courier* (Pittsburgh, PA), Letter to the Editor, Jan. 31, 1942, 3, https://www.newspapers.com/clip/33240765 /james-g-thompsons-letter-to-the/.

"There is no doubt . . .": ibid.

Chapter 8: Eleanor Roosevelt

"General Henry Arnold, chief . . .": Morris J. MacGregor, "Defense Studies—Integration of the Armed Forces, 1940–1965," Center of Military History, United States Army, (Washington, DC, 1981), 27, https:// history.army.mil/html/books/050/50-1-1/cmhPub_50-1-1.pdf.

"She used her 'My Day' column . . .": Eleanor Roosevelt, "My Day," The Eleanor Roosevelt Papers Digital Edition, Dec. 5, 1956, https://www2.gwu .edu/~erpapers/myday/displaydocedits.cfm?_y=1956&_f=md003660.

"The day came . . . able to land safely, too.": "Anderson, Charles Alfred 'Chief': Father of African American Aviation/Pilot," National Aviation Hall of Fame, https://www.nationalaviation.org/our-enshrinees/ anderson-charles-alfred/.

Chapter 9: Lieutenant Davis

"Despite his Southern roots . . . not fail them.": Daniel L. Haulman, "A Tale of Two Commanders," *Air Power History*, Summer 2018, vol. 65, no. 2, 45–49. https://www.jstor.org/stable/26571113.

"He answered the silly . . . stick and rudder.'" George W. Bush, "Remarks on Presenting the Congressional Gold Medal to the Tuskegee Airmen," Government Publishing Office, Mar. 29, 2007, https://www.govinfo .gov/content/pkg/WCPD-2007-04-02/html/WCPD-2007-04-02-Pg387-3 .htm.

"Your job, take . . . your bombers.": Roy Chappell, "Roy Chappell describes how the Tuskegee Airmen led to the integration of the US Air Force," The HistoryMakers Digital Archive, interviewed by Larry Crowe, May 14, 2002, Session 1, Tape 3, Story 6, https://thehistorymakers.org.

"One Tuskegee Airman, Roy . . .": Roy Chappell, "Roy Chappell describes the planes used by bombers during World War II," The HistoryMakers Digital Archive, interviewed by Larry Crowe, May 14, 2002, Session 1, Tape 3, Story 9, https://thehistorymakers.org.

Chapter 10: Bombardiers

"This country is not . . .": Ernest E. Johnson, "Negro Fliers Seen Victims of General's Planned Segregation," *Pittsburgh Courier*, June 2, 1945, 5.

"The army had rules . . .": Major John D. Murphy, "The Freeman Field Mutiny: A Study in Leadership" (A Research Paper Presented to the Research Department Air Command and Staff College in Partial Fulfillment of the Graduation Requirements of ACSC, March 1997), Appendix A: Army Regulation 210-10, Paragraph 19, pg 32, https://apps.dtic.mil/sti/pdfs/ADA397891.pdf.

"In Major General Hunter's . . .": Lynn M. Homan and Thomas Reilly, *Black Knights: The Story of the Tuskegee Airmen*, Gretna, LA: Pelican Publishing Company, Jan. 2001, 199–200.

Chapter 11: Freeman Field

"I killed two of them . . .": Michael Hankins, "Mutiny at Freeman Field: The Tuskegee Airmen on Trial, Part 2," Smithsonian National Air and Space Museum, June 9, 2020, https://airandspace.si.edu/stories/editorial/mutiny-freeman-field-tuskegee-airmen-trial-part-2.

"Their wives could not . . .": Rick Davis, "The Fight for Equality," *Creighton University Magazine*, Summer 2000, 15, https://dspace2.creighton.edu/xmlui/handle/10504/110452.

"Hotesse was born in the town . . .": Juleyka Lantigua-Williams, "An Unknown Latino Tuskegee Airman Has Been Discovered," *The Atlantic*, Nov. 5, 2015, https://www.theatlantic.com/politics/archive/2015/11/unknown-latino-tuskegee-airman-discovered/433479/.

Chapter 12: Mutiny

"An initial group of three . . .": Ronald W. Wolf, "Black History Month: Stay Focused! Stick to It! Get It Done!" US Army, Feb. 25, 2020, https://www.army.mil/article/233012/black_history_month_stay_focused_stick_to_it_get_it_done.

"No one knew that . . . their goal.": Major John D. Murphy, "The Freeman Field Mutiny: A Study in Leadership" (A Research Paper Presented to the Research Department Air Command and Staff College in Partial Fulfillment of the Graduation Requirements of ACSC, March 1997), https://apps.dtic.mil/sti/pdfs/ADA397891.pdf.

"Second Lieutenant Roger . . .": Roger Terry, "Eyewitness to Jim Crow, Roger 'Bill' Terry Remembers," *PBS: Jim Crow History*, https://web.archive.org/web/20051027032849/http://www.jimcrowhistory.org/resources/narratives/Roger_Terry.htm.

"[W]e had always been . . .": Molly Hennessy-Fiske, "Airmen Plan to Attend Inauguration," *Los Angeles Times*, Jan. 18, 2009, B10., https://www .newspapers.com/clip/37178064/roger-c-terry/.

"The continuance of this . . .": Michael Hankins, "Mutiny at Freeman Field: The Tuskegee Airmen on Trial, Part 2," Smithsonian Air and Space Museum, June 9, 2020, https://airandspace.si.edu/stories/editorial /mutiny-freeman-field-tuskegee-airmen-trial-part-2.

"Assignment of Housing . . .": Major John D. Murphy, "The Freeman Field Mutiny: A Study in Leadership" (A Research Paper Presented to the Research Department Air Command and Staff College in Partial Fulfillment of the Graduation Requirements of ACSC, March 1997), Appendix E: Base Regulation 85-2, pp. 37–39, https://apps.dtic.mil/sti /pdfs/ADA397891.pdf.

"Others drafted their own . . .": Michael Hankins, "Mutiny at Freeman Field"

"Lieutenant David A. Smith . . .": David A. Smith, "David A. Smith describes the Freeman Field mutiny, pt. 1," The HistoryMakers Digital Archive, interviewed by Shawn Wilson, Apr. 19, 2006, Session 1, Tape 3, Story 6, https://thehistorymakers.org.

"Lieutenant Quentin P. Smith . . .": "Quentin Smith Collection, (AFC/2001/001/03001)", Veterans History Project: American Folklife Center, Library of Congress, interviewed by Timothy Sanders, audio file, https://memory.loc.gov/diglib/vhp/bib/loc.natlib.afc2001001.03001.

"If I go up here and . . .": Hiram Little, "Hiram Little remembers the Freeman Field Mutiny, pt. 1," The HistoryMakers Digital Archive, interviewed by Denise Gines, Sept. 10, 2007, Session 1, Tape 3, Story 7, https://thehistorymakers.org.

Chapter 13: The 101 Club

"I wanted to go to med school . . .": Dr. James B. Williams, "Dr. James Williams describes his legal defense during the Freeman Field Mutiny," The HistoryMakers Digital Archive, interviewed by Larry Crowe, July 16, 2008, The HistoryMakers Digital Archive, Session 1, Tape 4, Story 5, https://thehistorymakers.org.

"The letters called each man . . .": Nicole Poletika, "Blacks Must Wage Two Wars: The Freeman Field Uprising & WWII Desegregation," *Indiana History Blog*, July 31, 2017, https://blog.history.in.gov /blacks-must-wage-two-wars-the-freeman-field-uprising-wwii -desegregation/.

"I thought what we were . . .": Rick Davis, "The Fight for Equality," *Creighton University Magazine*, Summer 2000, 14, https://dspace2 .creighton.edu/xmlui/handle/10504/110452.

"The board assigned to judge . . .": George Levi Knox III, "George Levi Knox III describes his father's role in the Freeman Field mutiny," The HistoryMakers Digital Archive, interviewed by Larry Crowe, Mar. 29, 2005, Session 1, Tape 2, Story 1, https://thehistorymakers.org.

Chapter 14: War's End

"Lieutenant Colonel Benjamin . . .": "New Deal at Godman," *The Journal and Guide*, June 23, 1945, Home Edition, vol. XLVI, no. 25, [From the Benjamin O. Davis Jr. Collection—[Godman Field] News clippings (Transcribed and Reviewed by Digital Volunteers)]

"The white folks, they were . . .": Roger Terry, "Eyewitness to Jim Crow, Roger 'Bill' Terry Remembers," *PBS: Jim Crow History*, https://web.archive.org/web/20051027032849/http://www.jimcrowhistory.org/resources/narratives/Roger_Terry.htm.

"Nobody cared much . . .": John D. Stevens, "From the Back of the Foxhole: Black Correspondents in World War II." *Journalism Monographs*, Feb. 1973, no. 27, http://files.eric.ed.gov/fulltext/ED096675.pdf.

"According to Brooks . . .": ibid.

"A scholar at CUNY . . .": Juleyka Lantigua-Williams, "An Unknown Latino Tuskegee Airman Has Been Discovered," *The Atlantic*, Nov. 5, 2014, https://www.theatlantic.com/politics/archive/2015/11/unknown-latino-tuskegee-airman-discovered/433479/.

"This is a fact . . .": Ted Wood, "Citizen Editor Promises to Print Record of 477th as Community Protests Article Slurring Outfis [sic]," *Ohio State News*, Columbus, OH, Feb. 2, 1946, 2, https://digital-collections.columbuslibrary.org/digital/collection/african/id/2591.

"One riot at Freeman Field . . .": "Ohio Capital Opposes Transfer of 477th pilots," *The Chicago Defender*, Feb. 9, 1946.

"An inspection report in 1948 . . .": Brenda Payton, "Tuskegee Airmen finally receive their recognition," *East Bay Times* (San Francisco Bay Area), Apr. 3, 2007, https://www.eastbaytimes.com/2007/04/03/tuskegee-airmen-finally-receive-their-recognition/.

"I used to love to watch . . .": George Levi Knox III, "George Levi Knox III describes the sights, sounds and smells of his childhood," The HistoryMakers Digital Archive, interviewed by Larry Crowe, Mar. 29, 2005. Session 1, Tape 2, Story 4, https://thehistorymakers.org.

"Everywhere on the base . . .": "Call for Military Memorabilia: The Tuskegee Airmen and Lockbourne," *Ohio History Connection*, Feb. 12, 2016, https://www.ohiohistory.org/learn/collections/history/history-blog/2016/february-2016/call-for-military-memorabilia-the-tuskegee-airmen.

"Tuskegee Airmen often came . . .": Carolyn Thompson, "Tuskegee Airmen Receive Congressional Gold Medal," AP News, Nov. 11, 2016, https://apnews.com/article/6a71f49864f546f188d43aeb605bc5c7.

"It actually got to . . .": Randy Roughton, "Black Airmen turn racism, bigotry, into opportunity," Air Force News Service, Feb. 4, 2014, https://www.af.mil/News/Article-Display/Article/473251/black-airmen-turn-racism-bigotry-into-opportunity/.

"Folk artist Woody Guthrie . . .": Chris Lamb, "The police beating that opened America's eyes to Jim Crow's brutality," *The Conversation*, Feb. 11, 2016, https://theconversation.com/the-police-beating-that-opened-americas-eyes-to-jim-crows-brutality-53932.

"In February 1946 . . .": DeNeen L. Brown, "A Black WWII veteran was beaten and blinded, fueling the civil rights movement," *Washington Post*, Mar. 31, 2021. https://www.washingtonpost.com/history/2021/03/31/isaac-woodard-truman-integration-military/.

"According to a 1946 news . . .": ibid.

"I was born a white man . . .": Lamb, "The police beating."

"All the defense attorney . . .": Brown, "A Black WWII veteran."

"He attacked Jim Crow laws . . .": District Court Eastern District of South Carolina, "Dissenting opinion in *Harry Briggs, Jr., et al. v. R. W. Elliott, Chairman, et al.,*" National Archives and Records Administration: Records of District Courts of the United States:1865–1902, filed June 23, 1951, https://catalog.archives.gov/id/279306.

"It is my joy that . . .": Linda Klein, "'Grandma,' 3 Sons Run Clinic—Her Dream Come True," *Chicago Tribune*, June 27, 1964.

Chapter 15: The War for Health Care

"His report claimed Blacks needed . . .": Abraham Flexner, "Medical Education in the United States and Canada," Carnegie Foundation for the Advancement of Teaching, (New York, 1910), Bulletin No. 4, http://archive.carnegiefoundation.org/publications/pdfs/elibrary/Carnegie_Flexner_Report.pdf.

"I had a little bird . . .": Sara Francis Fujimura, "Purple Death: The Great Flu of 1918," *Perspectives in Health: The Magazine of the Pan American Health Organization*, Nov. 3, 2003, vol. 8, no. 3, https://www3.paho.org/English/DD/PIN/Number18_article5.htm.

"I went for an interview . . .": Dr. James B. Williams, "Dr. James Williams describes his and his brothers' early medical careers," The HistoryMakers Digital Archive, interviewed by Larry Crowe, July 16, 2008, Session 1, Tape 4, Story 8, https://thehistorymakers.org.

"Beginning in 1845 . . .": Shankar Vedantam, Maggie Penman, Jennifer Schmidt, Chloe Connelly, and Tara Boyle, "Remembering Anarcha, Lucy, and Betsey: The Mothers of Modern Gynecology," *NPR Hidden Brain*, audio file, Feb. 7, 2017, https://www.npr.org/2017/02/07/513764158/remembering-anarcha-lucy-and-betsey-the-mothers-of-modern-gynecology.

"Nevertheless, doctors like . . .": Vanessa N. Gamble, "'There Wasn't a Lot of Comforts in Those Days': African Americans, Public Health, and the 1918 Influenza Epidemic," *Public Health Reports,*2010; 125 (Suppl. 3):114–122, https://www.ncbi.nlm.nih.gov/pmc/articles/PMC2862340/.

"JB went to the school's . . .": Dr. James B. Williams, "Dr. James Williams recalls applying to medical schools," The HistoryMakers Digital Archive, interviewed by Larry Crowe, July 16, 2008, Session 1, Tape 5, Story 1, https://thehistorymakers.org.

"Willeen was described as . . .": Brenda Payton Jones, "Brenda Payton Jones describes her mother's family background," The HistoryMakers Digital Archive, interviewed by Loretta Henry, Apr. 3, 2006, Session 1, Tape 1, Story 3, https://thehistorymakers.org.

Chapter 16: The National Medical Association

"One day when he walked . . .": Rick Davis, "The Fight for Equality," *Creighton University Magazine*, Summer 2000, 16,19, https://dspace2.creighton.edu/xmlui/handle/10504/110452.

"The AMA has demonstrated . . .": Harriet A. Washington, "Apology Shines Light on Racial Schism in Medicine," *New York Times*, Essay, July 29, 2008, https://www.nytimes.com/2008/07/29/health/views/29essa.html.

"You ought to build it here . . .": Dr. James B. Williams, "Dr. James Williams recalls Dr. Lawrence A. Nixon," The HistoryMakers Digital Archive, interviewed by Larry Crowe, July 16, 2008, Session 1, Tape 1, Story 7, https://thehistorymakers.org.

"The doctrine of . . .": United States Supreme Court, *"Brown v. Board of Education,"* National Archives and Records Administration: Records of the Supreme Court of the United States, 1772–2007, decided: May 17, 1954, https://catalog.archives.gov/id/1656510.

"With the deadline for . . .": National Medical Association Website, "History," accessed Dec. 3, 2020,https://www.nmanet.org/page/History.

"First, as a reminder . . .": "History of the Imhotep National Conference on Hospital Integration," *Journal of the National Medical Association,* Jan., 1962, vol. 54, no. 1, 117.

"Segregation today . . .": George C. Wallace, "Inaugural Address of Governor George C. Wallace," Alabama Department of Archives and History, Jan. 14, 1963, https://digital.archives.alabama.gov/digital/collection /voices/id/2952.

"Their victims included . . .": "Children's Crusade," National Museum of African American History & Culture, https://nmaahc.si.edu/blog /childrens-crusade.

"For seven years we have . . .": Harriet A. Washington, "Apology Shines Light on Racial Schism in Medicine," *New York Times,* Essay, July 29, 2008, https://www.nytimes.com/2008/07/29/health/views/29essa.html.

"He came over and kidded me . . .": Rick Davis, "The Fight for Equality," *Creighton University Magazine,* Summer 2000, 17, https://dspace2 .creighton.edu/xmlui/handle/10504/110452.

"We are confronted primarily . . .": John F. Kennedy, "Civil Rights Announcement, 1963," *American Experience,* June 11, 1963, https:// www.pbs.org/wgbh/americanexperience/features/jfk-civilrights/.

Chapter 17: Medical Practice

"When civil rights icon . . . for the listening FBI operatives.": Rick Davis, "The Fight for Equality," *Creighton University Magazine,* Summer 2000, 17–19, https://dspace2.creighton.edu/xmlui /handle/10504/110452.

"His love of flying . . . health care to community members.": "Flying Black Medics Dramatize Cairo's Poor Health Care," *Jet* magazine, Mar. 5, 1970, 16–23.

Chapter 18: Mutiny's Final Acts

"The 104 officers involved . . .": James C. Warren, *The Freeman Field Mutiny,* San Rafael, CA: Donna Ewald 1995, 210.

"My father didn't have much . . .": Steve Ramirez, "Dr. James Williams, Las Crucen Who Served with Tuskegee Airmen, Dies," *Las Cruces Sun News* (Las Cruces, NM), Nov. 27, 2016.

"Richard Terry, the only man convicted . . ." Nicole Poletika, "Blacks Must Wage Two Wars: The Freeman Field Uprising & WWII Desegregation," *Indiana History Blog*, July 31, 2017, https://blog.history.in.gov/blacks -must-wage-two-wars-the-freeman-field-uprising-wwii-desegregation/.

"I benefited from what you . . .": George W. Bush, "Remarks on Presenting the Congressional Gold Medal to the Tuskegee Airmen," Government Publishing Office, Mar. 29, 2007, https://www.govinfo.gov/content /pkg/WCPD-2007-04-02/html/WCPD-2007-04-02-Pg387-3.htm.

"I would like to offer . . .": ibid.

"I never thought I would see . . .": Steve Ramirez, "Dr. James Williams, Las Crucen Who Served with Tuskegee Airmen, Dies," *Las Cruces Sun News* (Las Cruces, NM), Nov. 27, 2016.

"That was really special . . .": ibid.

"This is the meaning of . . ." Barack Obama, "President Barack Obama's Inaugural Address," Jan. 21, 2009, https://obamawhitehouse.archives .gov/blog/2009/01/21/president-barack-obamas-inaugural-address.

"Obama gave a good . . ." Steve Ramirez, "Dr. James Williams, Las Crucen Who Served with Tuskegee Airmen, Dies," *Las Cruces Sun News* (Las Cruces, NM), Nov. 27, 2016.

Chapter 19: Legacy

"As a good parent . . .": Dr. James B. Williams, "Dr. James Williams describes how he would like to be remembered," The HistoryMakers Digital Archive, interviewed by Larry Crowe, July 16, 2008, Session 1, Tape 6, Story 9, https://thehistorymakers.org.

"Then, Brenda remembers . . .": Brenda Payton Jones, "Brenda Payton Jones recalls experiencing racial discrimination in Hyde Park," The HistoryMakers Digital Archive, interviewed by Loretta Henry, Apr. 3, 2006, Session 1, Tape 2, Story 1, https://thehistorymakers.org.

"She can remember a girl . . .": ibid.

"I guess I would be . . .": ibid.

"There have been many . . .": History.com editors, "Police kill two members of the Black Panther Party," A&E Television Networks, Nov. 13, 2009, https://www.history.com/this-day-in-history /police-kill-two-members-of-the-black-panther-party.

". . . always remembered what . . .": Brenda Payton Jones, "Brenda Payton Jones describes her political involvement as a teenager," The

HistoryMakers Digital Archive, interviewed by Loretta Henry, Apr. 3, 2006, Session 1, Tape 2, Story 6, pt. 1, https://thehistorymakers.org.

"Dr. James Buchanan Williams II . . . got started in 1993.": Dr. James B. Williams II, colorectal surgeon and son of Dr. James B. Williams, interview with author, 2021.

"My father did not talk . . .": Steve Ramirez, "Dr. James Williams, Las Crucen Who Served with Tuskegee Airmen, Dies," *Las Cruces Sun News* (Las Cruces, NM), Nov. 27, 2016.

"He didn't make out like . . .": ibid.

PHOTOGRAPH AND ILLUSTRATION CREDITS

Photos ©: ii–iii: H. Charles McBarron/National Guard; iv–v: Hiraman/iStock/Getty Images; 2: Everett/Shutterstock; 5: New Mexico State University Library, Archives and Special Collections; 14–15: Library of Congress; 17: National Archives; 20–21: Kharbine-Tapabor/Shutterstock; 24: H. Charles McBarron/National Guard; 25: Collection of the Smithsonian National Museum of African American History and Culture, Gift of Gina R. McVey, Granddaughter; 26: National Archives; 27: Alpha Stock/Alamy Stock Photo; 33: Library of Congress; 34: Chicago History Museum, ICHi-040222; 43: Chicago History Museum, ICHi-040052, Jun Fujita, photographer; 45: Chicago History Museum, ICHi-065492, Jun Fujita, photographer; 52: Library of Congress; 56: BLM New Mexico; 60: Joseph C. Yaroch; 64–65: Library of Congress; 70: Courtesy of

Special Collections, University of Missouri Libraries; 74: Fotosearch/Getty Images; 83: www.donstivers .com; 85: National Museum of the United States Army, Scott Metzler; 86: Science History Images/Alamy Stock Photo; 87: GL Archive/Alamy Stock Photo; 100: Charles 'Teenie' Harris/Carnegie Museum of Art/Getty Images; 112–113: U.S. Air Force; 116–117: Afro American Newspapers/Gado/Getty Images; 119: National Archives; 120: National Archives; 123: U.S. Army; 126–127: National Archives; 128–129: U.S. Air Force; 131: U.S. Air Force; 134: Courtesy of the Williams family; 136: U.S. Air Force; 143: Indiana Historical Society, M0783; 145: Afro American Newspapers/Gado/Getty Images; 149: Afro American Newspapers/Gado/ Getty Images; 161: Timothy Molinari, Sr. & Jr./Freeman Army Field Museum; 165: U.S. Air Force; 166–167: Library of Congress; 174: Library of Congress; 184–185: Painted by Chris Hopkins; 188: U.S. Air Force/Tech. Sgt. Christopher Boitz; 194: Library of Congress; 205: From the collection of Michigan Medicine, University of Michigan, UMHS.30; 212–213: John Tweedle; 221:

Library of Congress; 230: Bettmann/Getty Images; 232–233: Cecil Stoughton/JFK Library; 235: U.S. Army/ Maj. Thomas Cieslak; 236: U.S. Army; 237: Courtesy of the Williams family; 239: Associated Press/AP Images; 242–243: Johnson Publishing Company Archive/ Courtesy Ford Foundation, J. Paul Getty Trust, John D. and Catherine T. MacArthur Foundation, Andrew W. Mellon Foundation and Smithsonian Institution; 258: Tribune Content Agency LLC/Alamy Stock Photo; 270: Hiraman/iStock/Getty Images.

ACKNOWLEDGMENTS

Five years ago, I was asked by members of the organization Moms of Black Boys United, Inc., to write a few vignettes about some Black mothers to use during Women's History Month. One of the women I chose to write about was Clara Belle Williams. By the time I finished researching and writing a page about that remarkable mother and educator, I was fascinated by her middle son, Dr. James Buchanan Williams. I want to acknowledge and thank that organization for getting me started on a journey that led me to someone so historically significant, and someone I lived so close to, I could have easily passed Dr. Williams and members of his family on the street a dozen times while growing up in Chicago. I only wish I had known about him when I was young.

I also want to thank Dr. James B. Williams II for the time he spent sharing information with me about his father. And to Wilhelmina Houston, a nurse and my sister, who talked to me about Dr. Charles Williams.

Thank you to my agent, Andrea Somberg, who has guided and pushed me and my writing for years, even when I strayed. And to my editor at Scholastic, Lisa Sandell, who fell in love with Dr. James Williams the way I did. She gave me valuable feedback all along the journey from manuscript to final product.

ABOUT THE AUTHOR

Barbara Binns is an African American author of contemporary, multicultural stories. She was born and raised on Chicago's South Side. She writes to attract and inspire readers with stories of "real boys growing into real men . . . and the people who love them."

Her books for middle grade and young adult readers include *Pull*, *Being God*, and *Courage*. Her writing has won an Oregon 2010 Reader's Choice Award and was chosen for the 2012 YALSA Quick Picks for Reluctant Readers list. In addition to writing, she volunteers with groups from students to senior citizens, and gives lectures and workshops to both experienced and aspiring authors.

As the eldest of five children, Barbara learned responsibility at an early age. Her eclectic career path includes work as a clinical chemist at the University of Chicago Hospitals, as a computer analyst for AT&T, and now as an author for her readers. She finds writing for young people an exercise in self-discipline and the perfect follow-up to her life as an adoptive parent and cancer survivor. She lives and writes in a suburb of Chicago.

You can find Barbara on Twitter at @barbarabinns, Facebook at @allthecolorsoflove, or on her website at babinns.com.